ZOMBIES HAVE ISSUES

GREG STONES

CHRONICLE BOOKS

SAN FRANCISCO

Library of Congress Cataloging-in-Publication Data
Stones, Greg.
  Zombies have issues / Greg Stones.
     pages cm
  ISBN 978-1-4521-3290-7
  1. Zombies—Humor. I. Title.

  PN6231.Z65S77 2014
  818'.602—dc23 ·

                        2013036173

Manufactured in China
Designed by Michael Morris

10 9 8 7 6 5 4 3 2

Chronicle Books LLC
680 Second Street
San Francisco, California 94107
www.chroniclebooks.com

Chronicle Books publishes distinctive books and gifts. From
award-winning children's titles, bestselling cookbooks, and
eclectic pop culture to acclaimed works of art and design,
stationery, andjournals, we craft publishing that's instantly
recognizable for its spirit and creativity. Enjoy our publishing
and become part of our community at www.chroniclebooks.com.

FSC
www.fsc.org
MIX
Paper from
responsible sources
FSC® C008047

ZOMBIES HAVE ISSUES WITH . . .

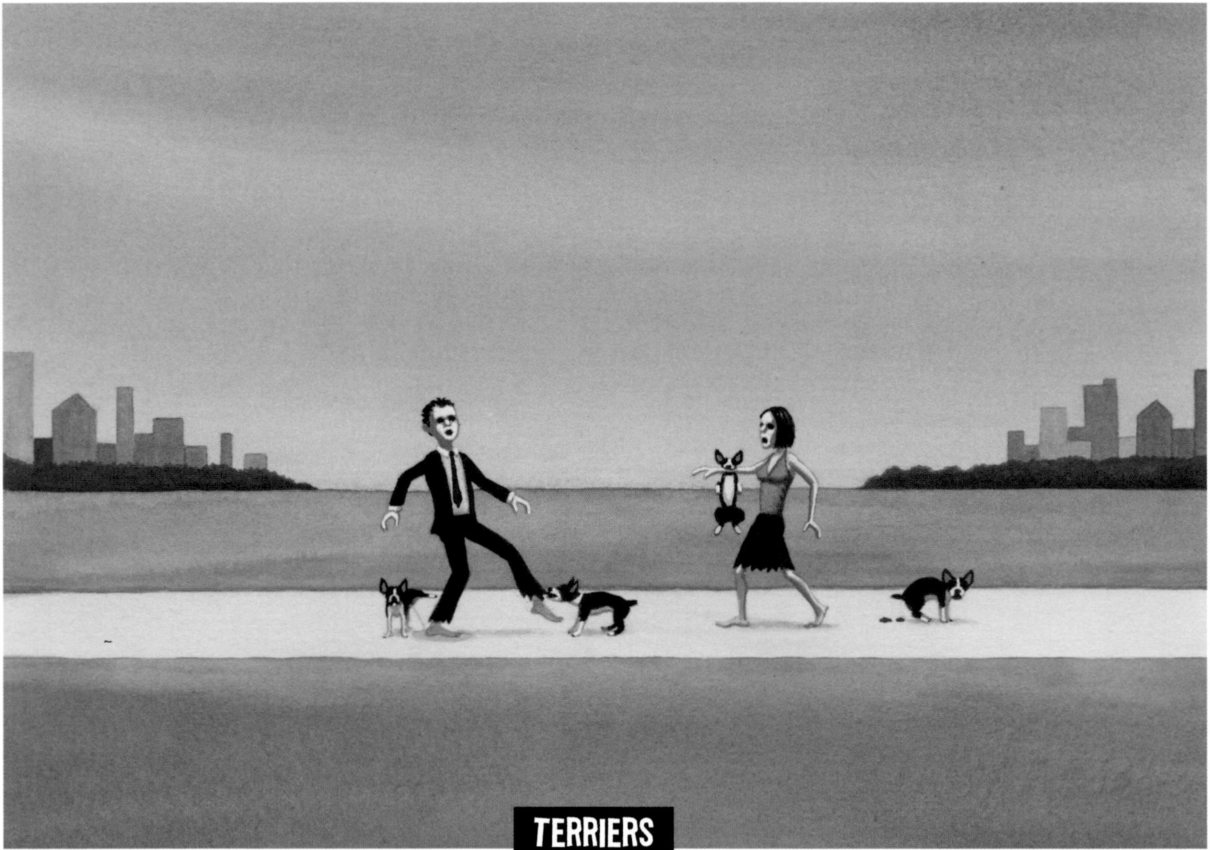

TERRIERS

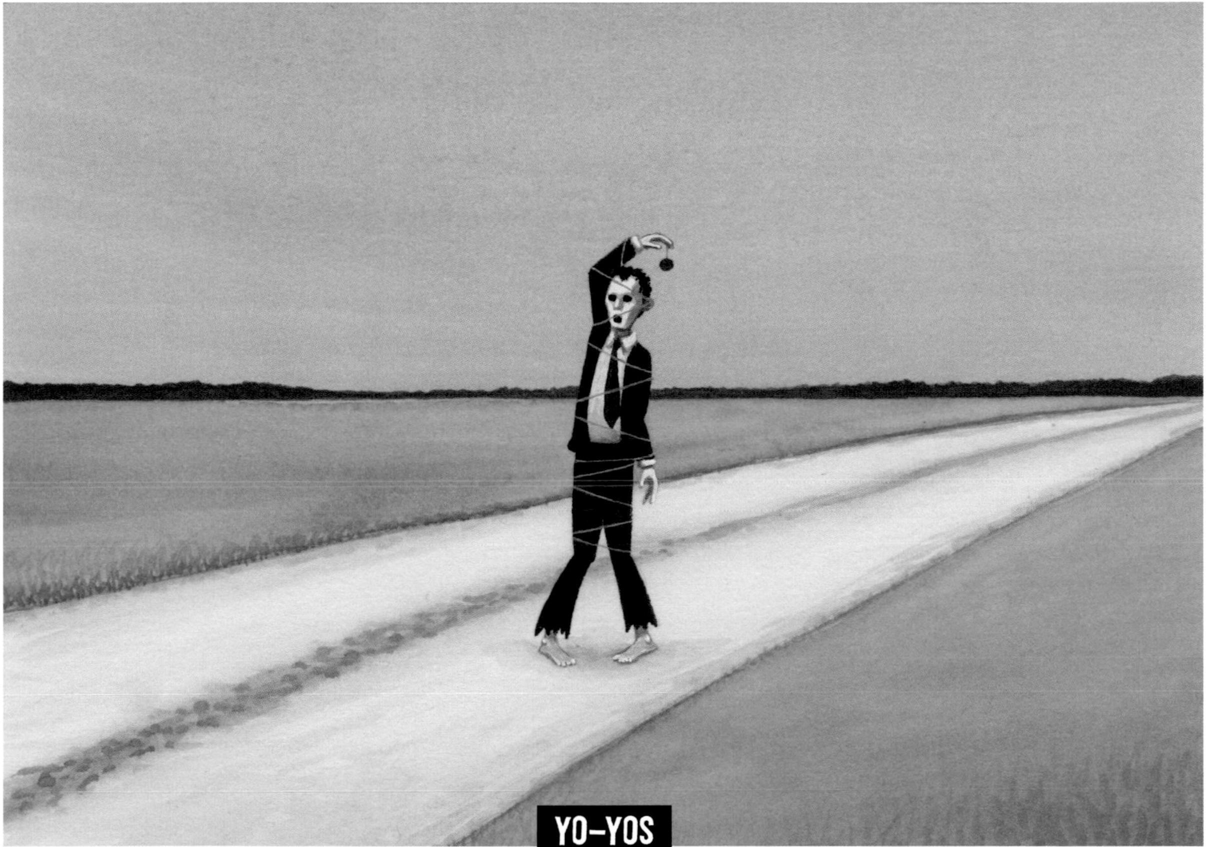

YO-YOS

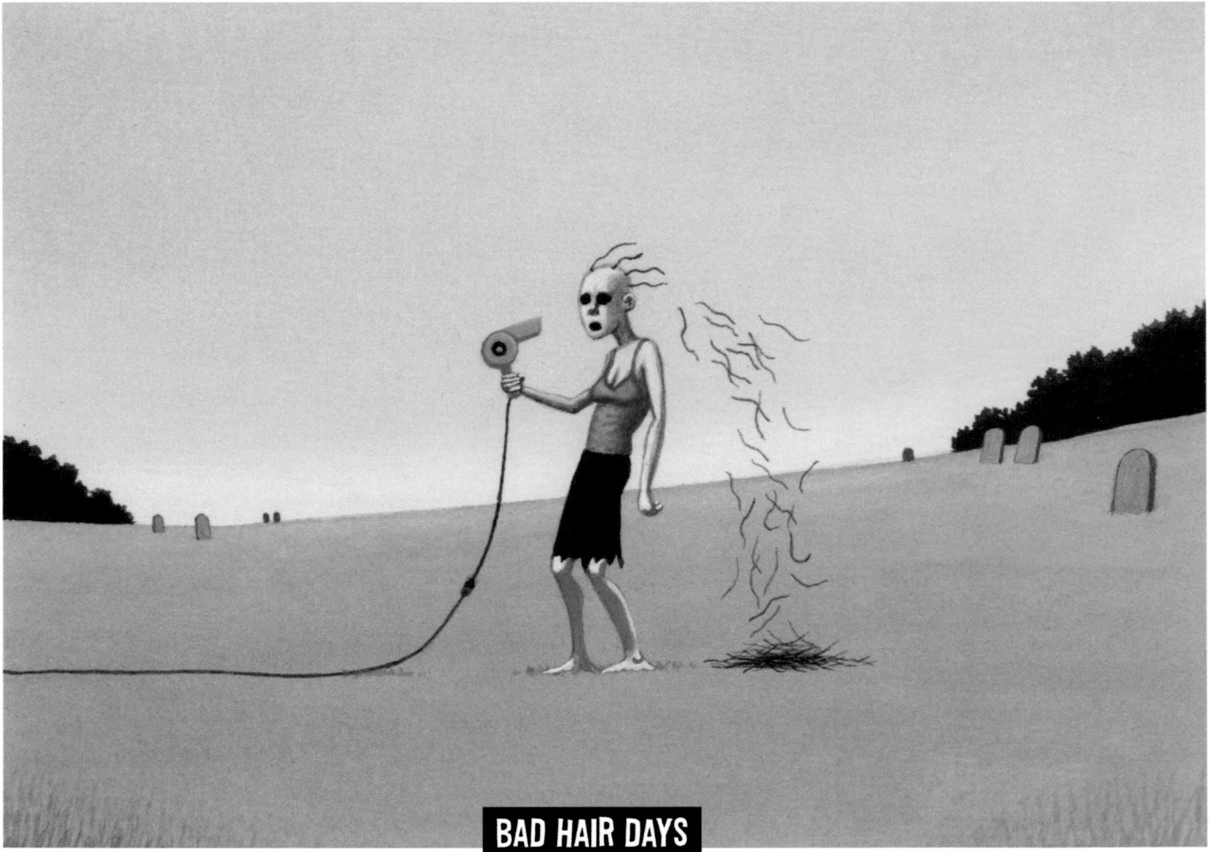

BAD HAIR DAYS

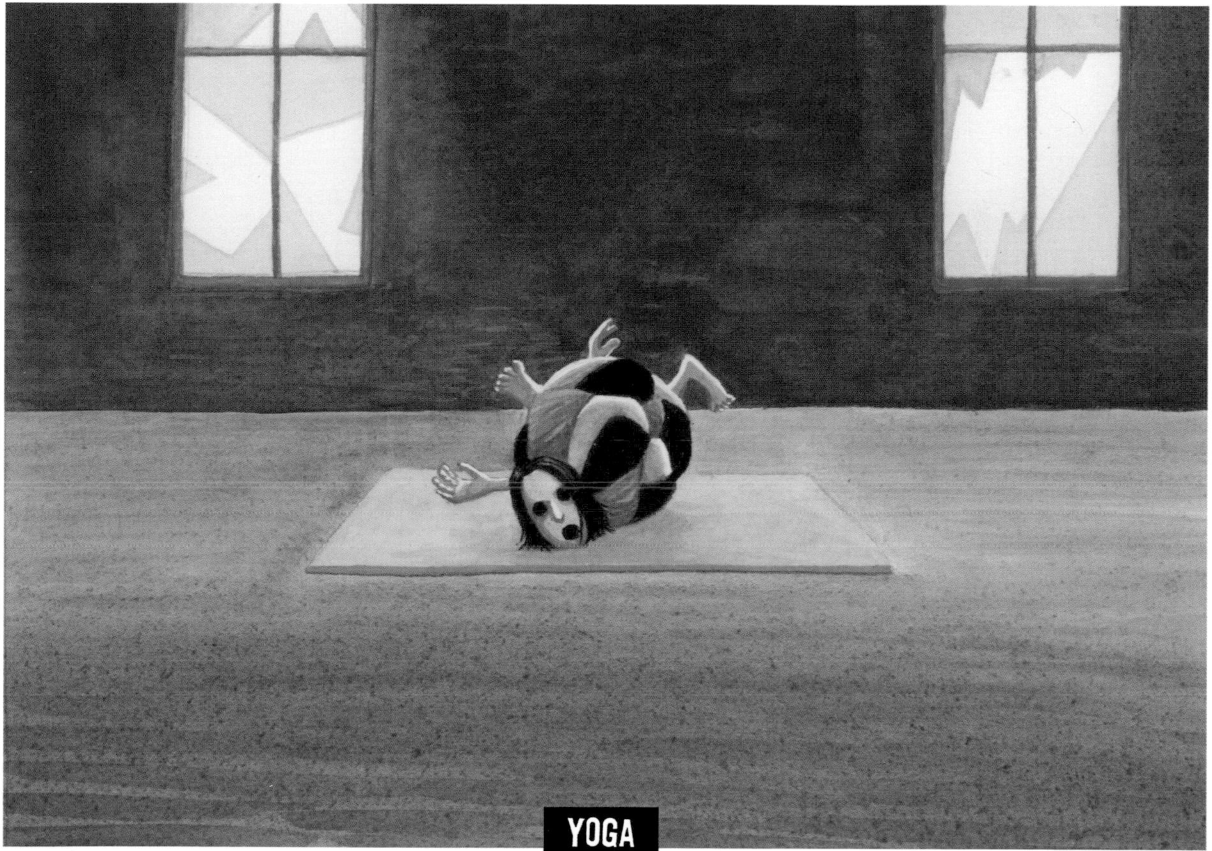

YOGA

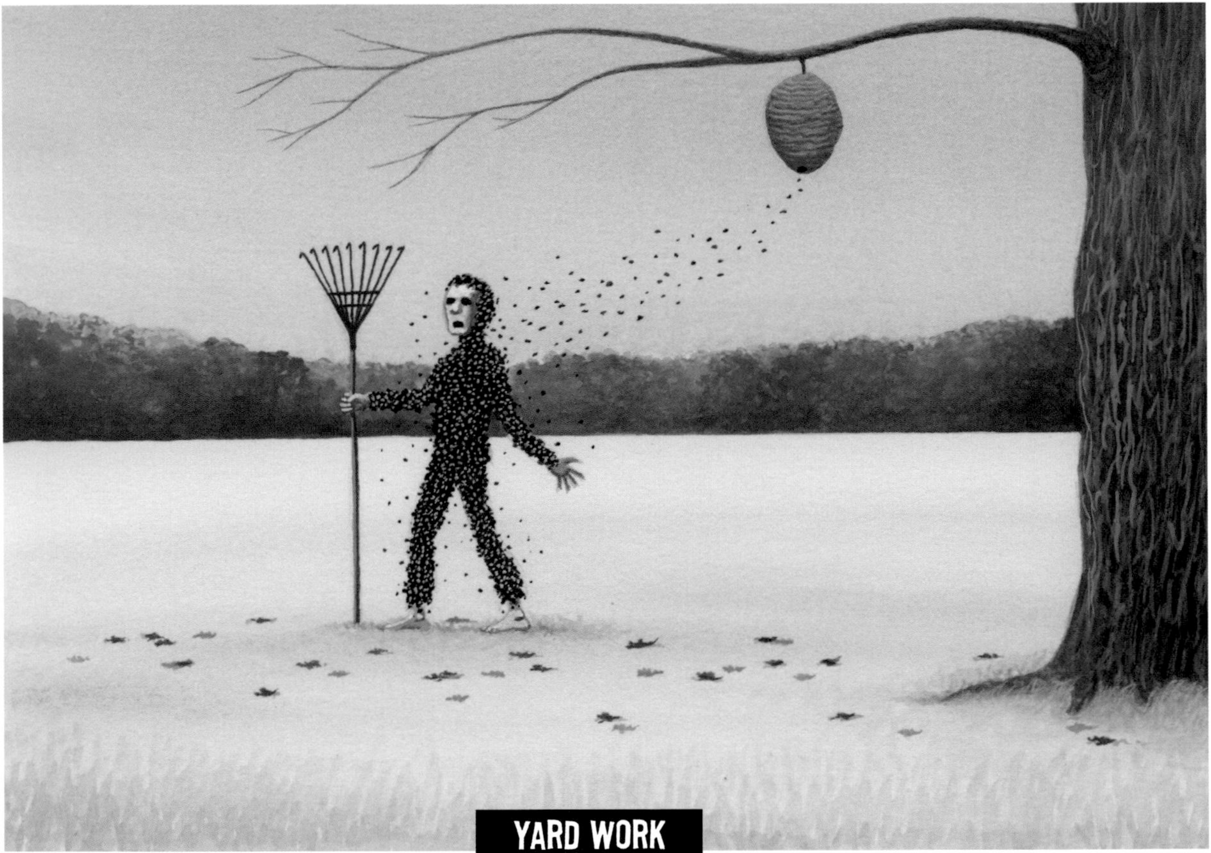

YARD WORK

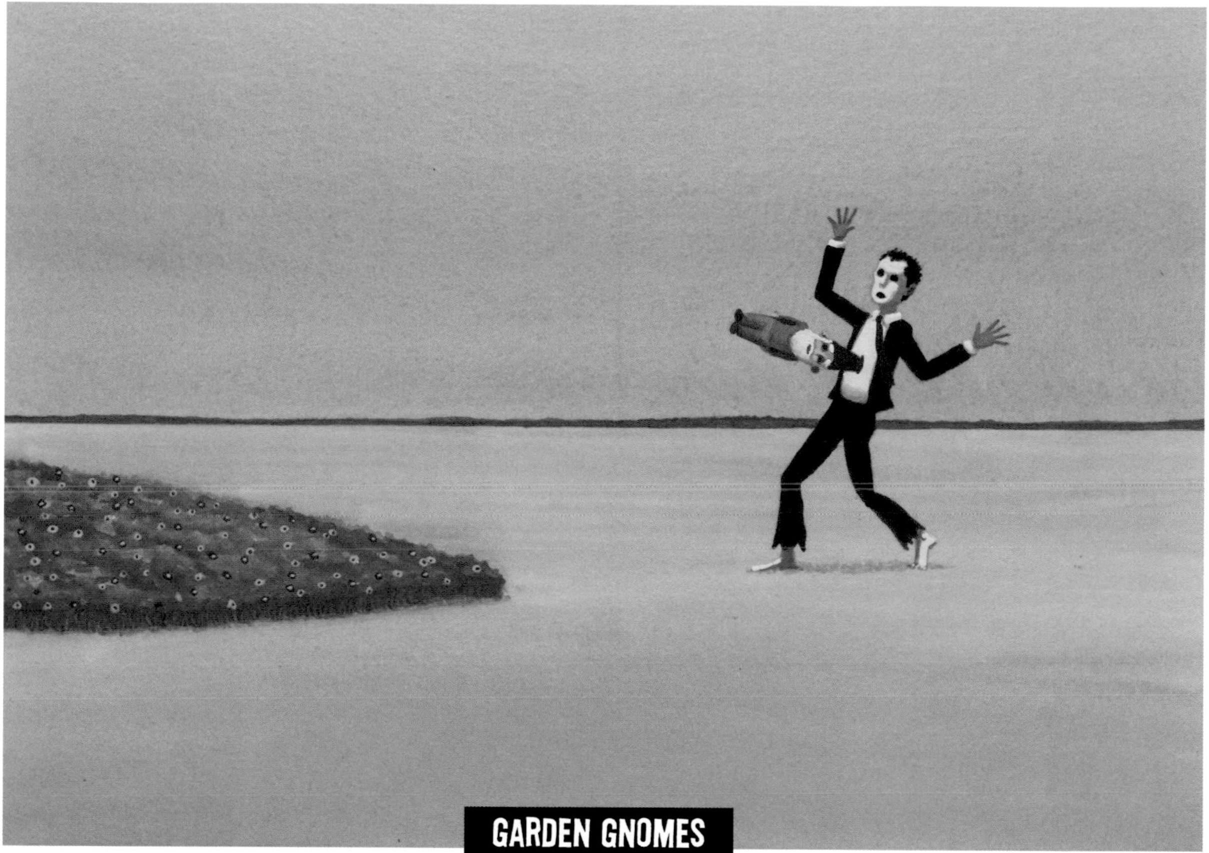

GARDEN GNOMES

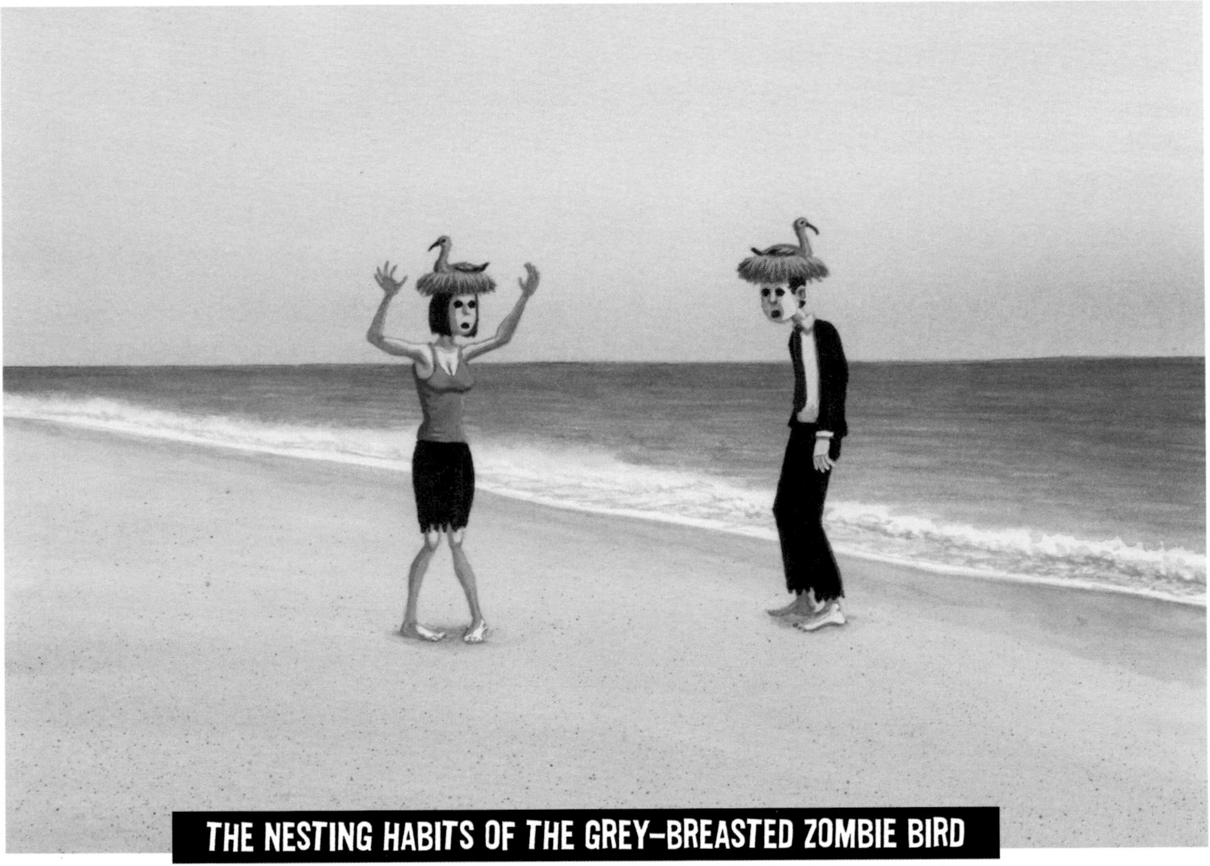

THE NESTING HABITS OF THE GREY-BREASTED ZOMBIE BIRD

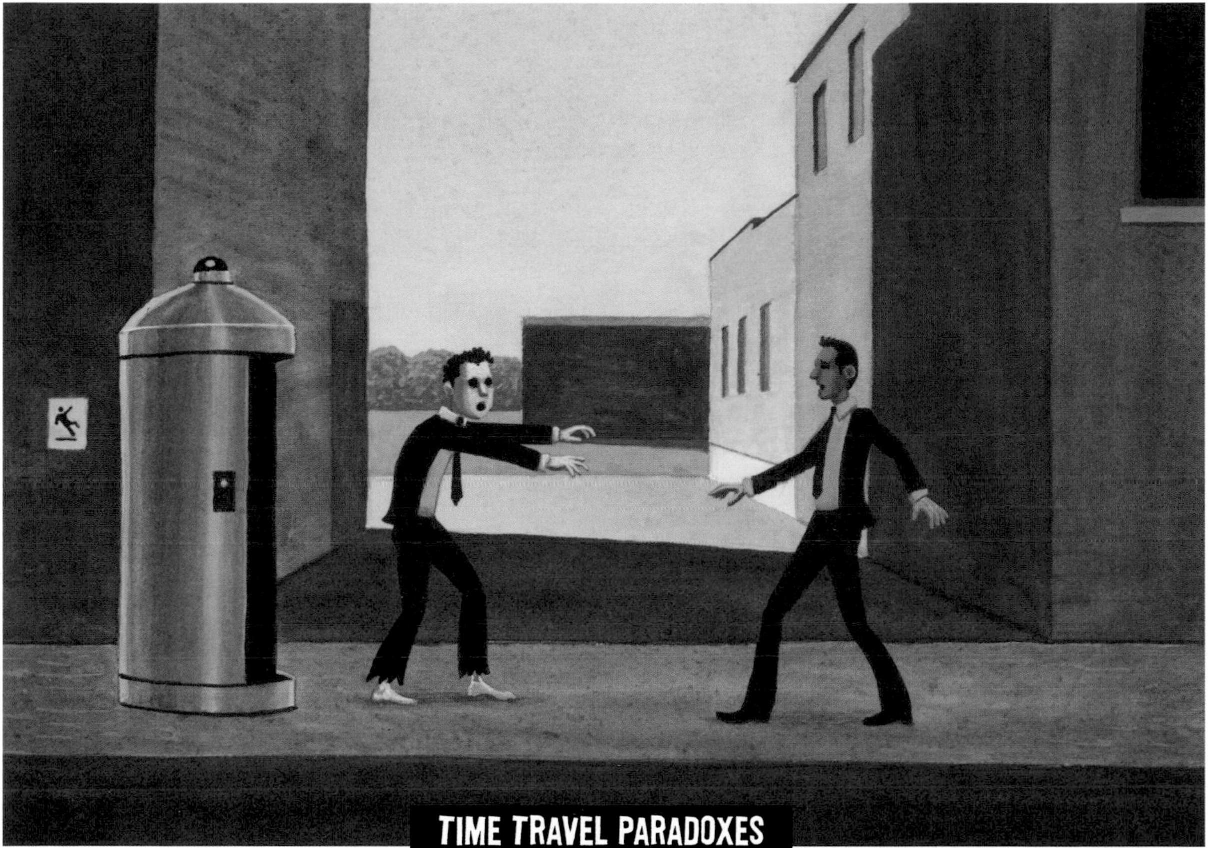

TIME TRAVEL PARADOXES

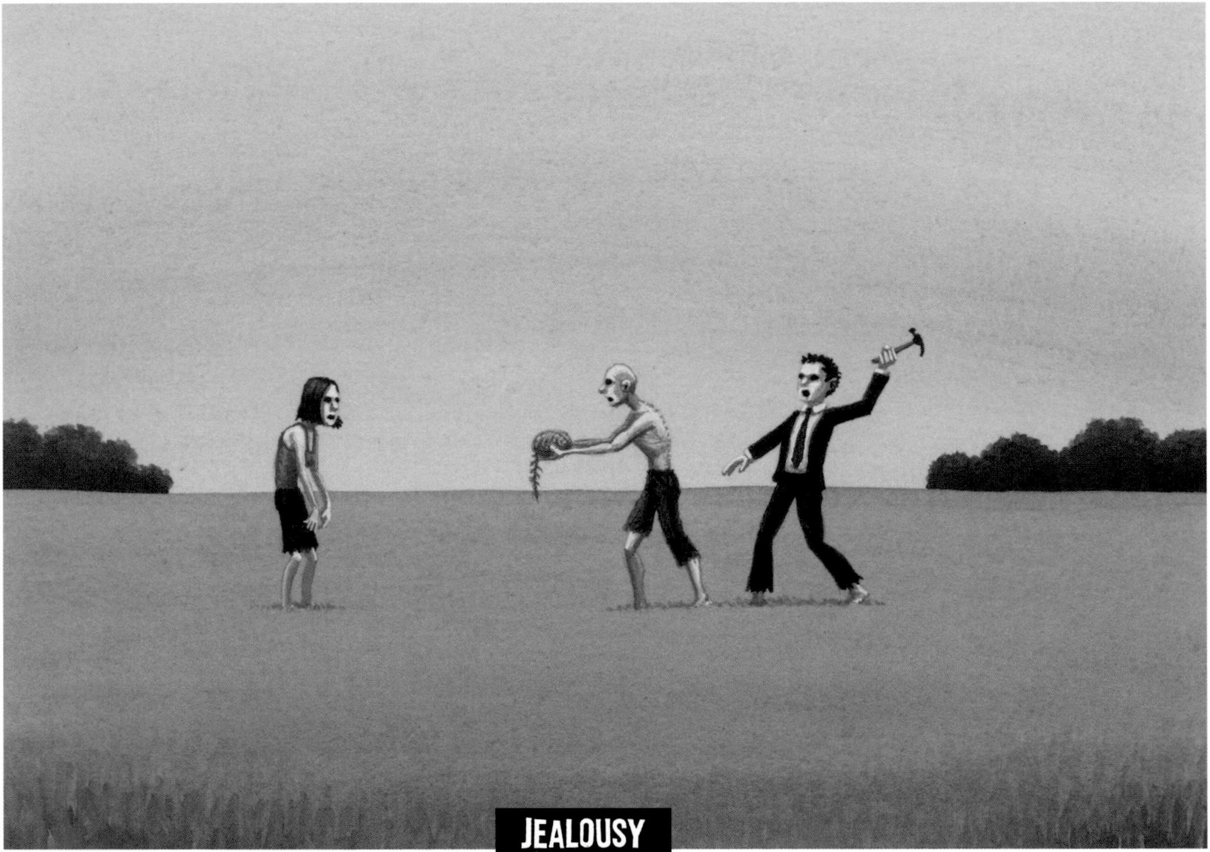

JEALOUSY

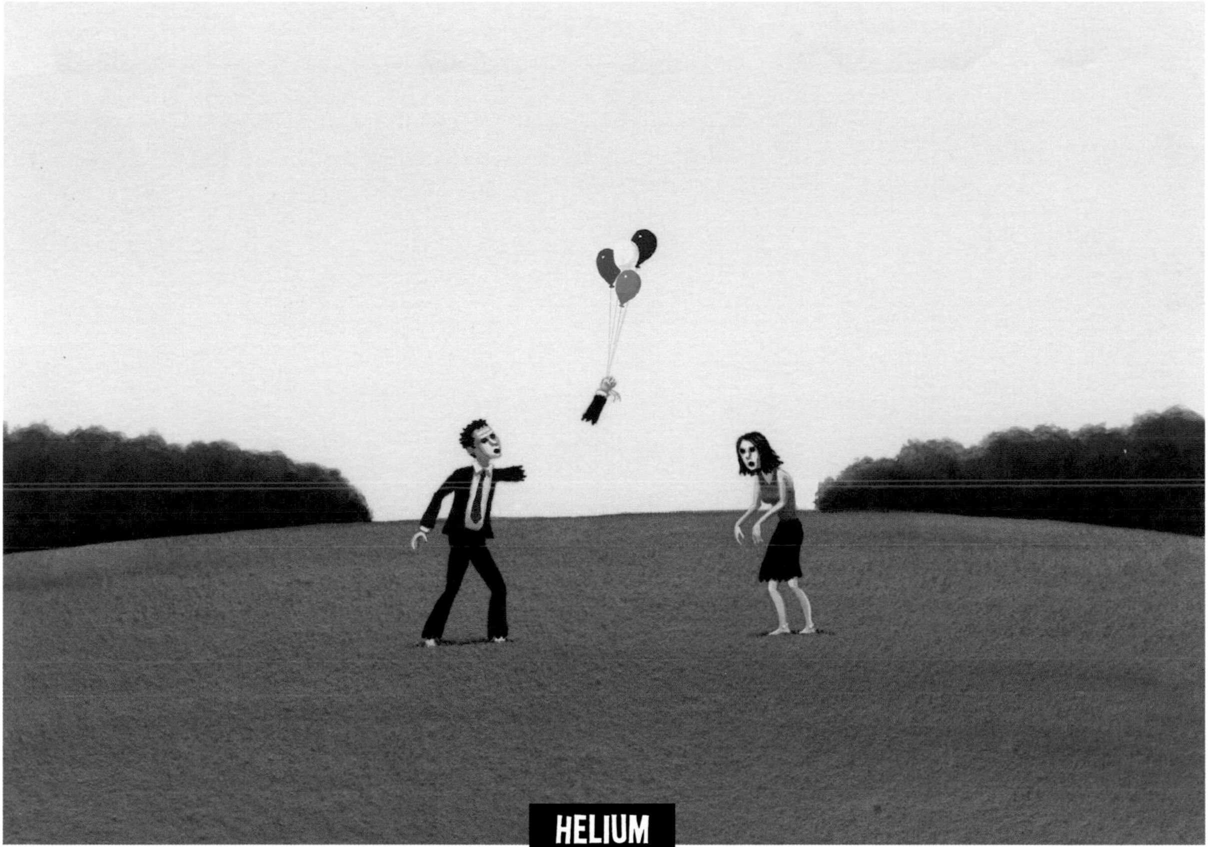

HELIUM

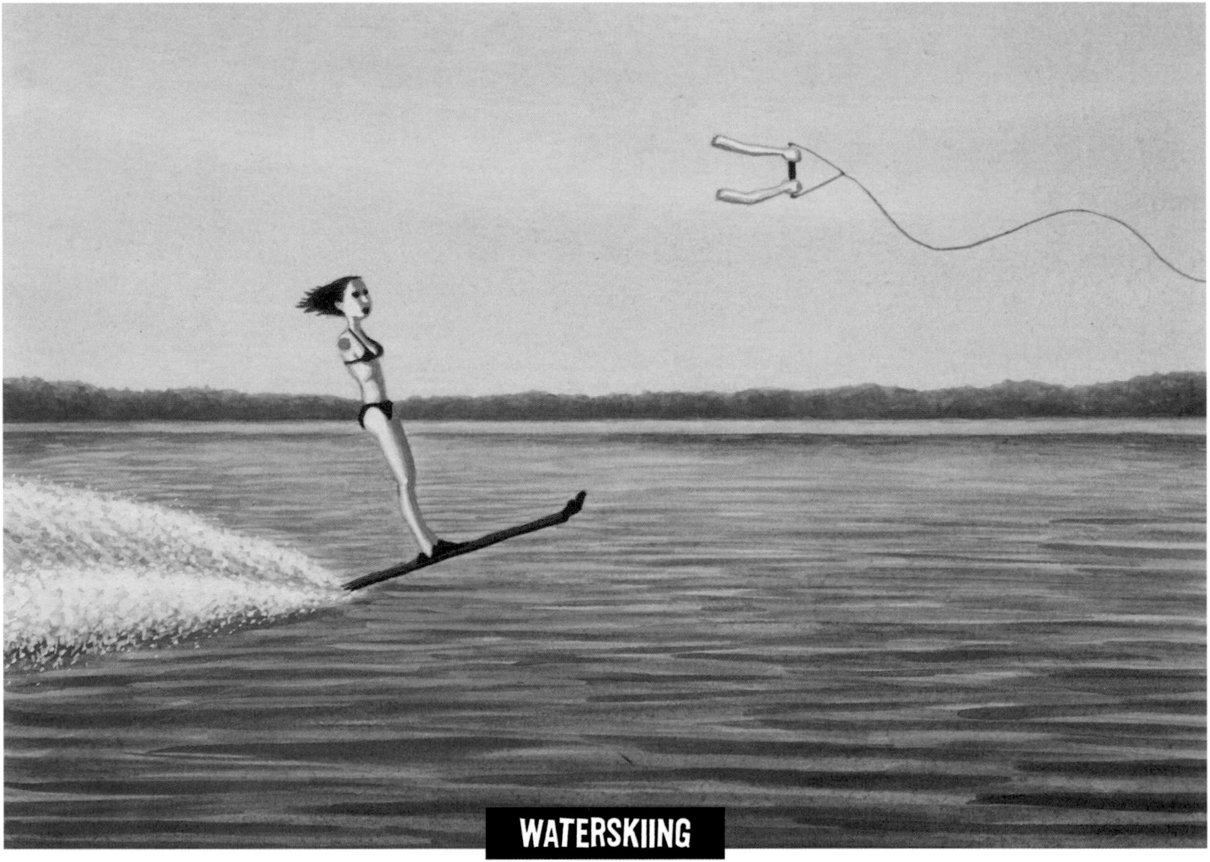

WATERSKIING

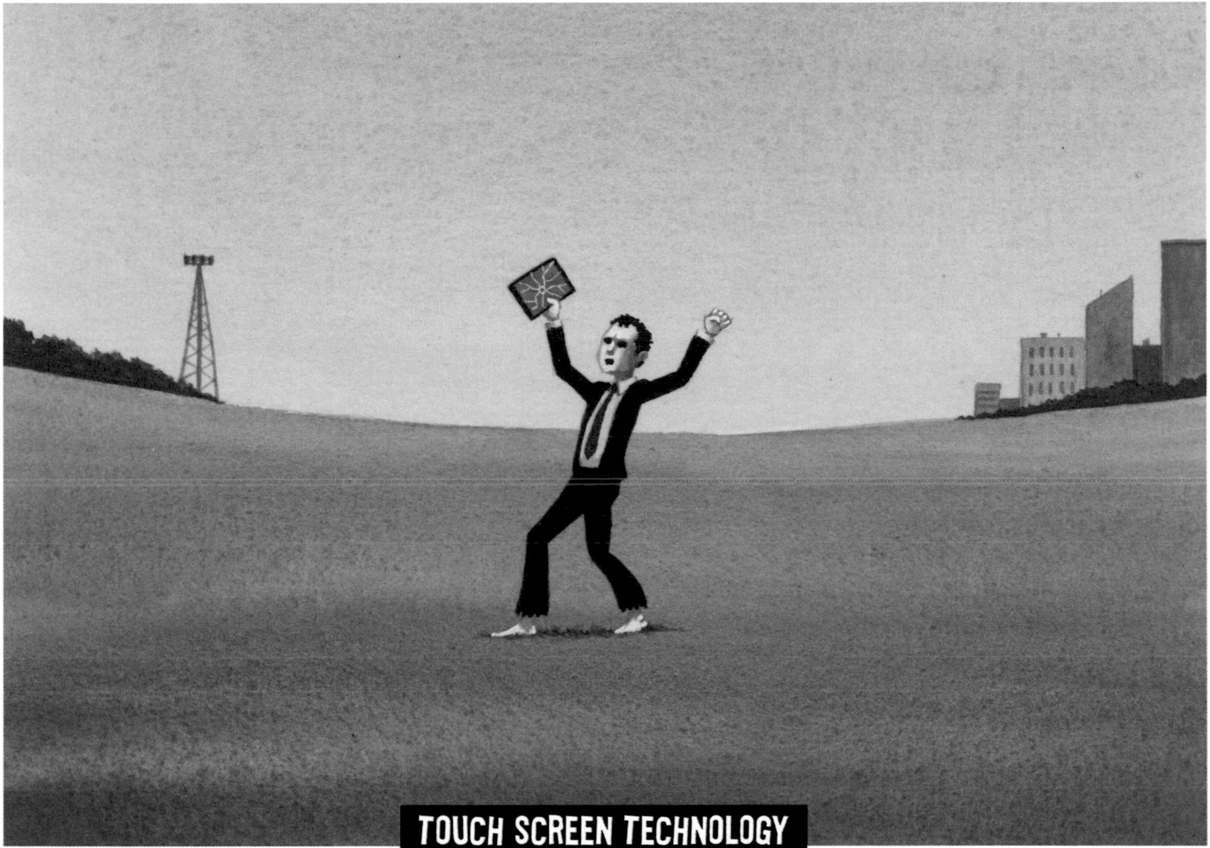

TOUCH SCREEN TECHNOLOGY

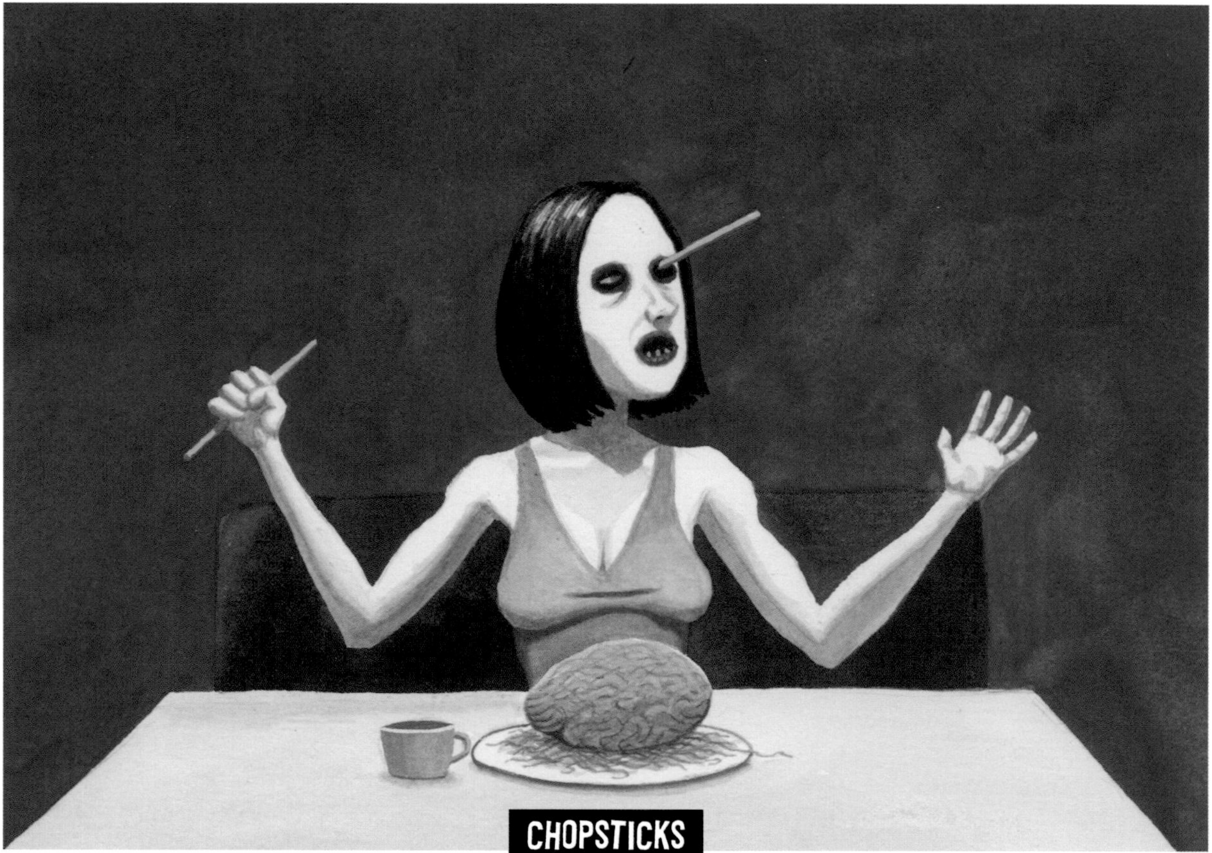

CHOPSTICKS

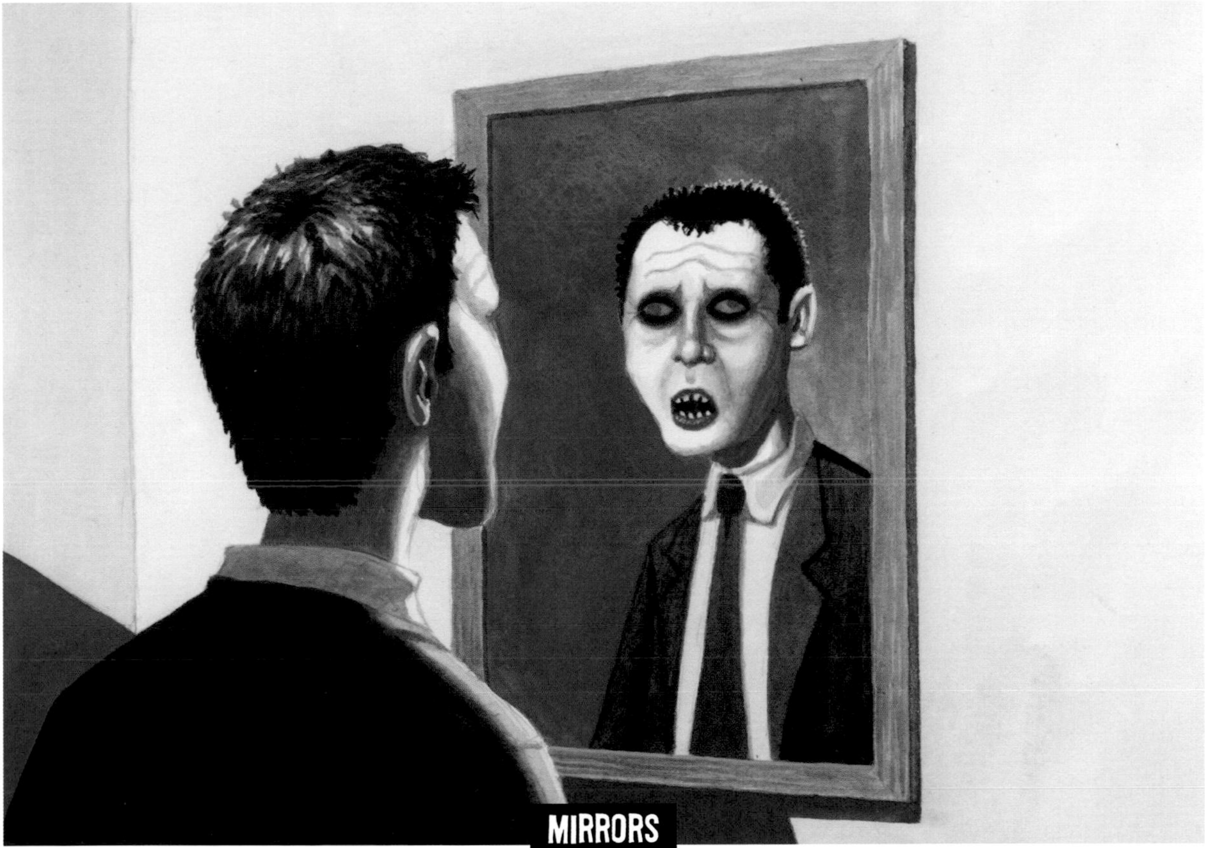

MIRRORS

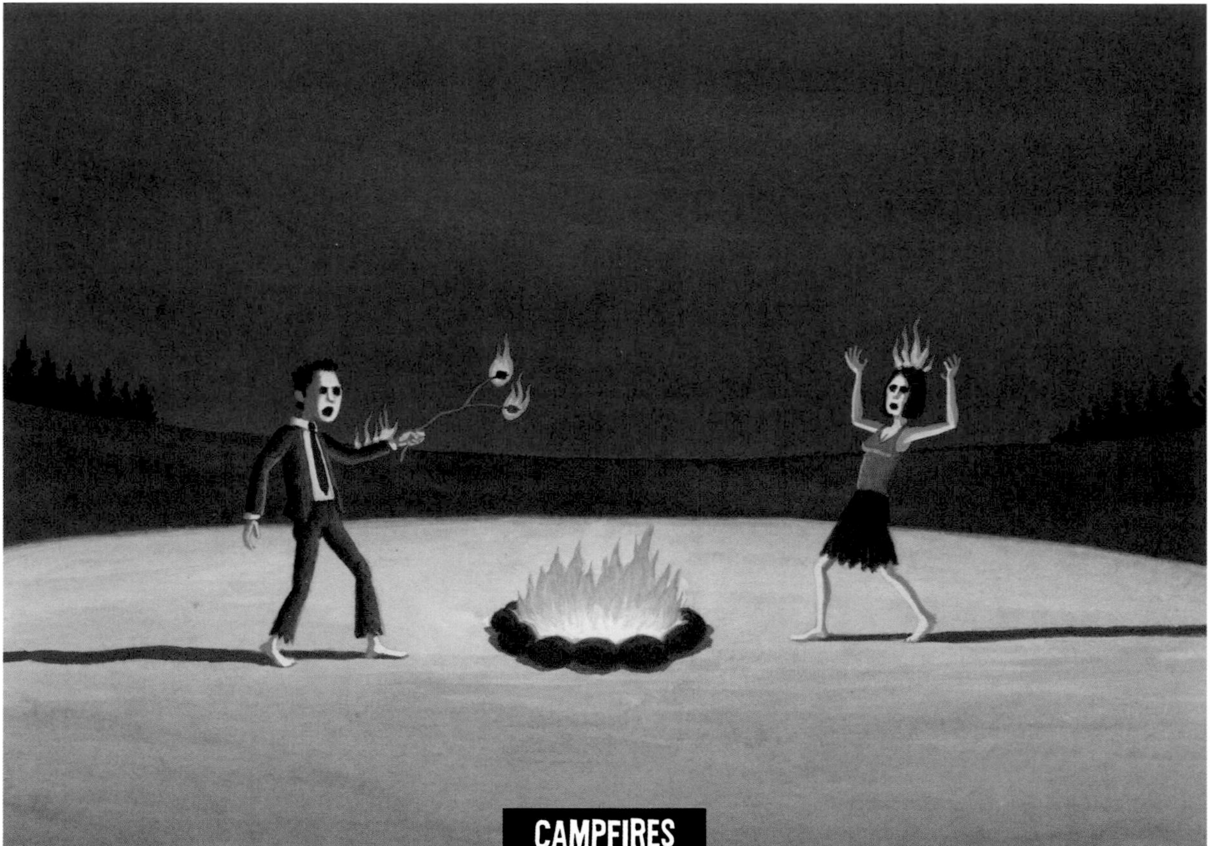

CAMPFIRES

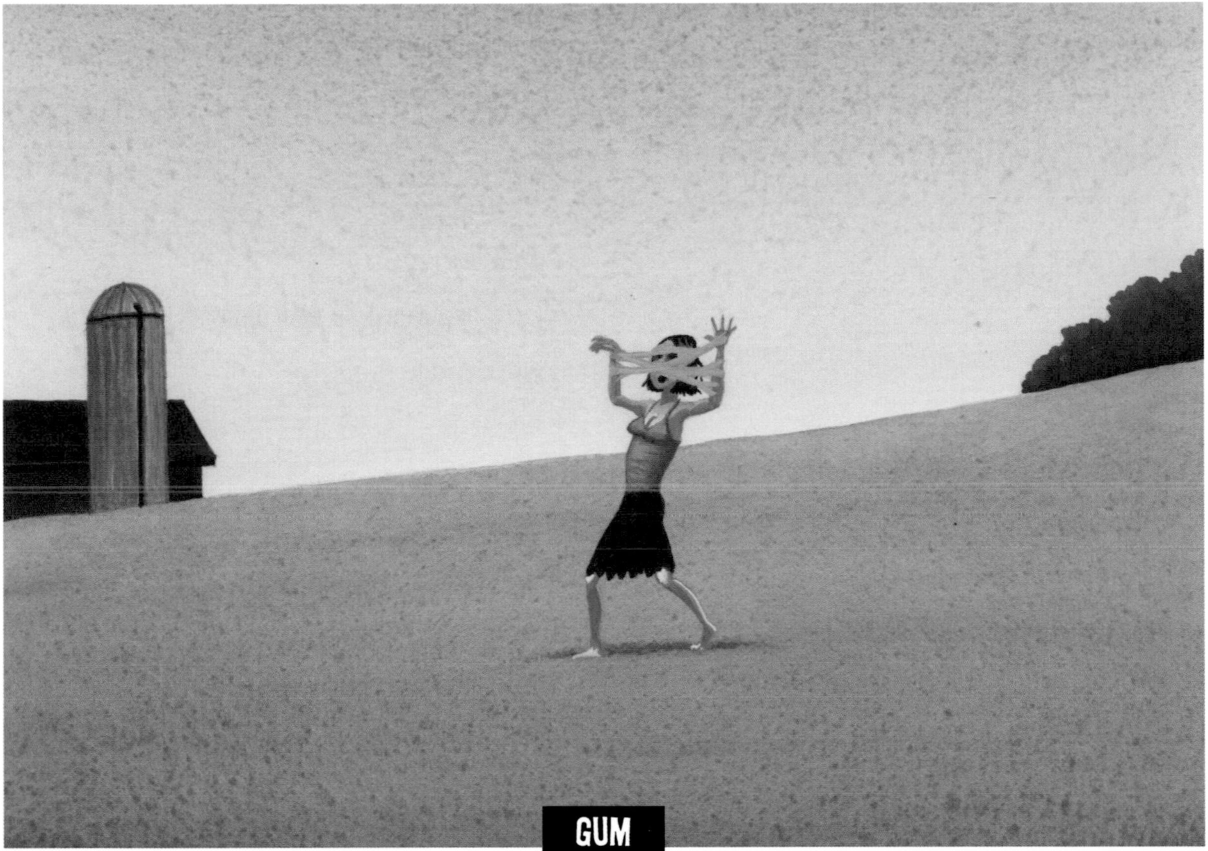

GUM

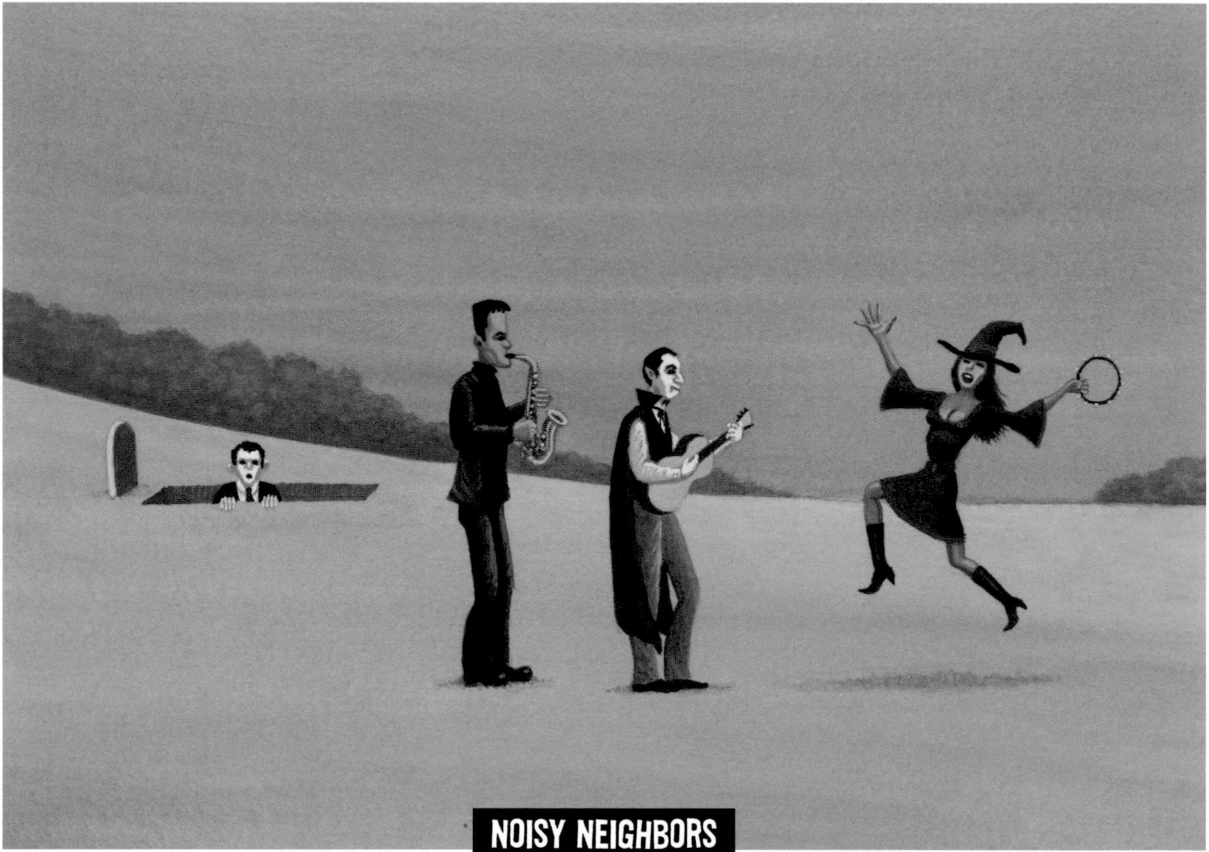

NOISY NEIGHBORS

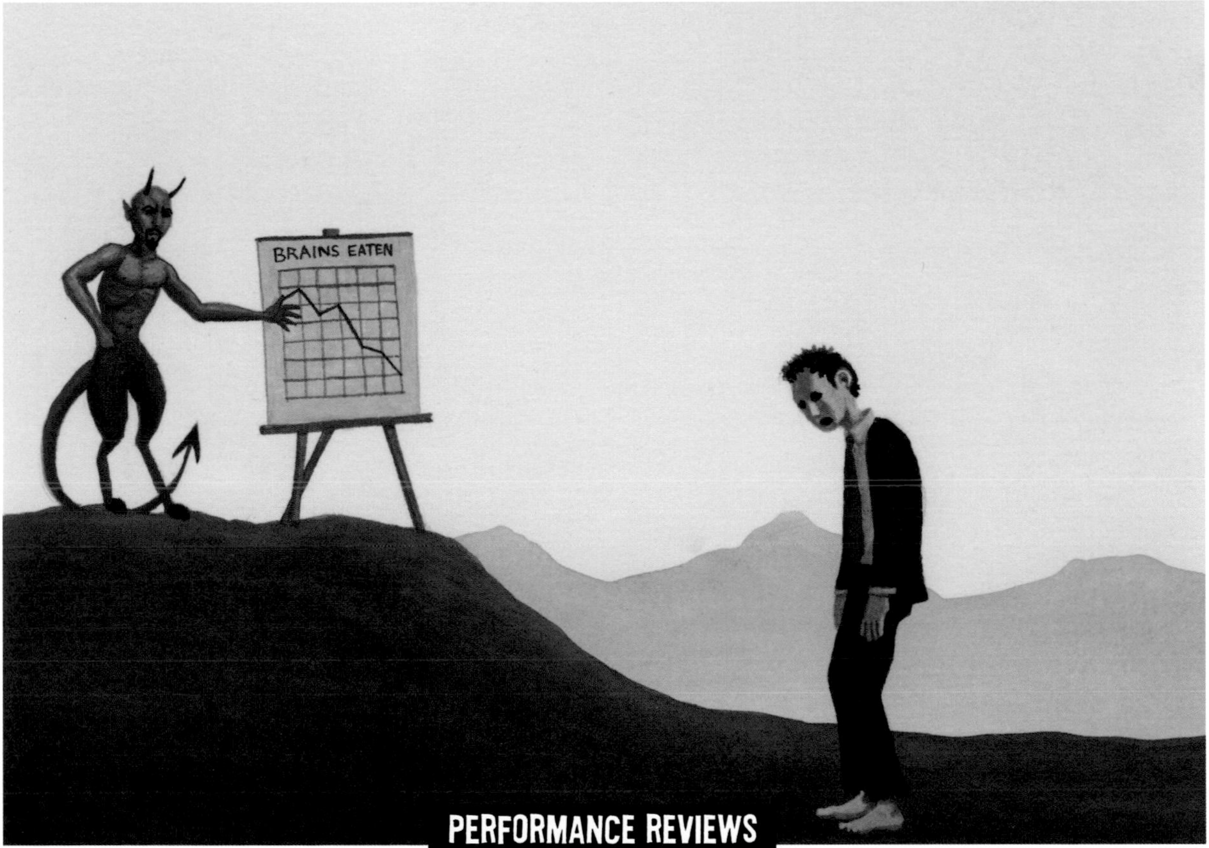
BRAINS EATEN

PERFORMANCE REVIEWS

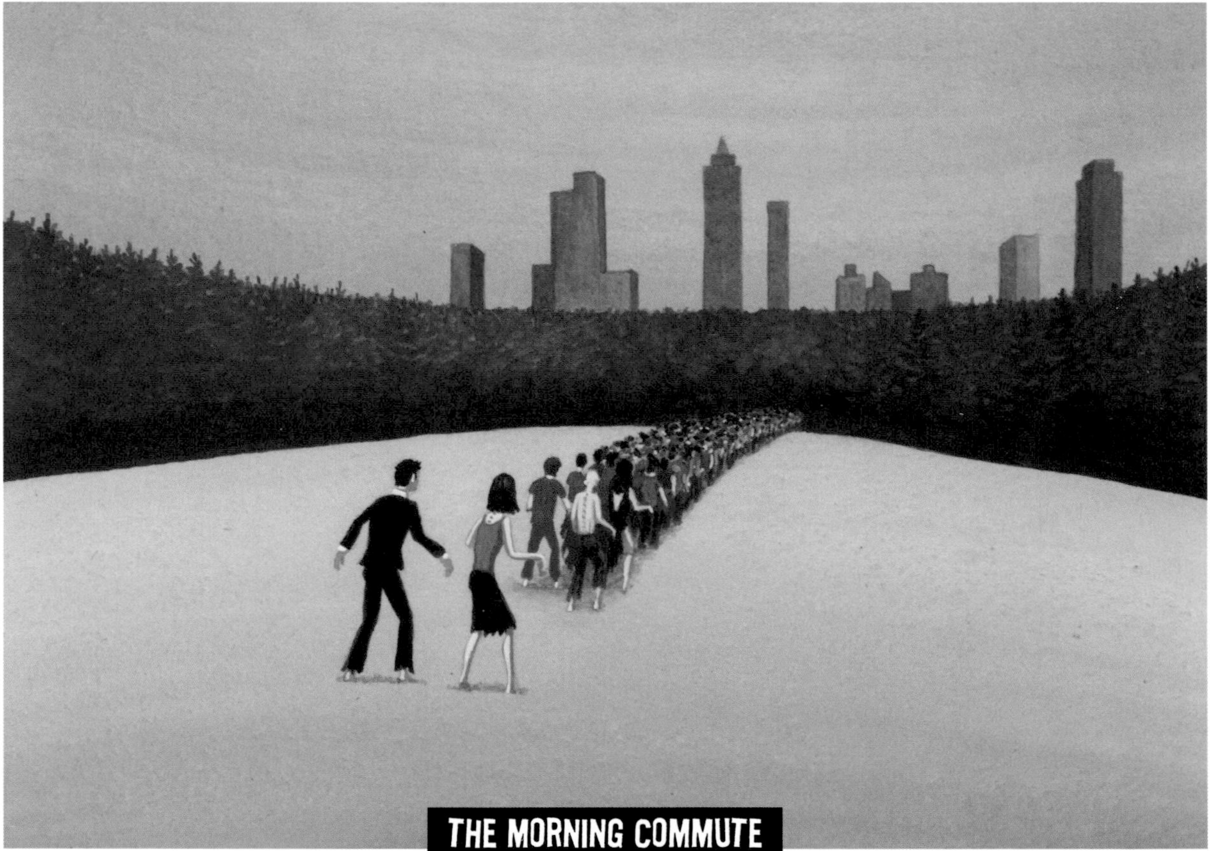

THE MORNING COMMUTE

ZOMBIES KIND OF ENJOY . . .

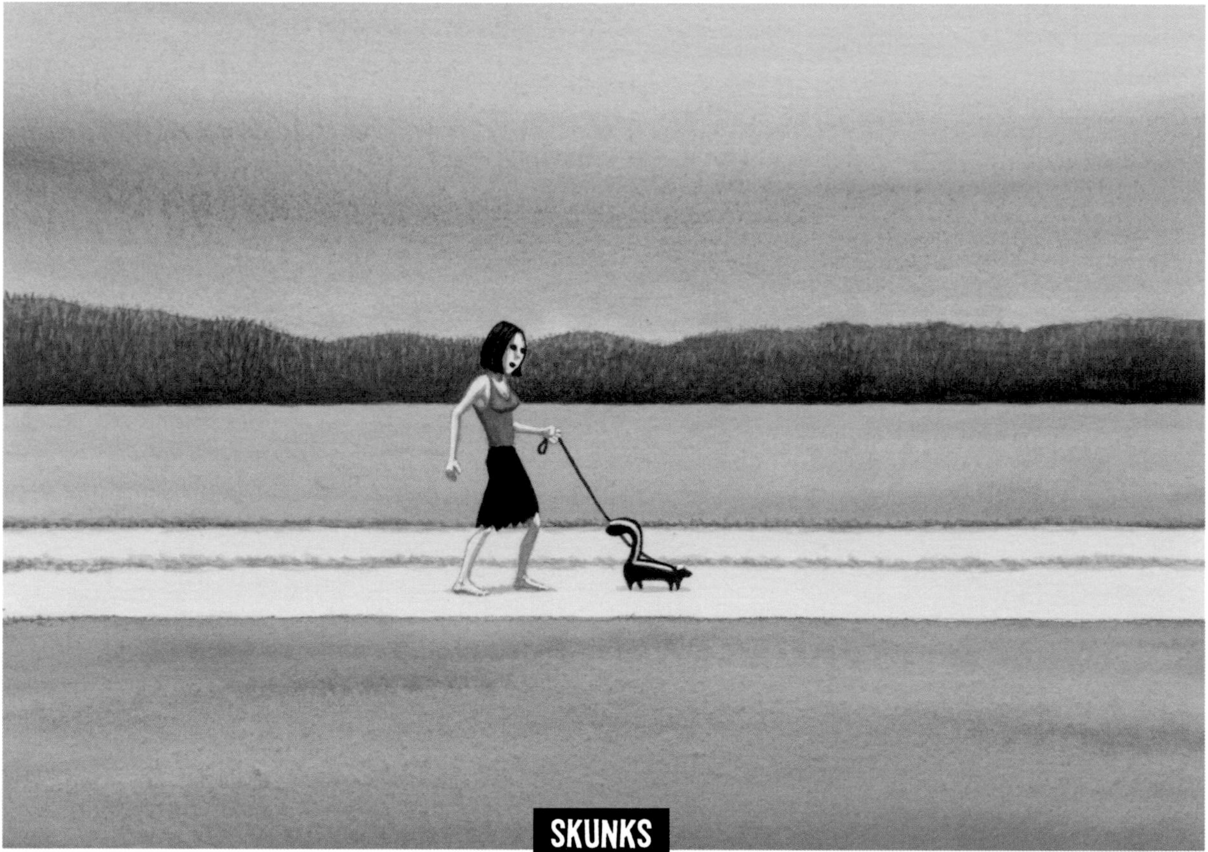

SKUNKS

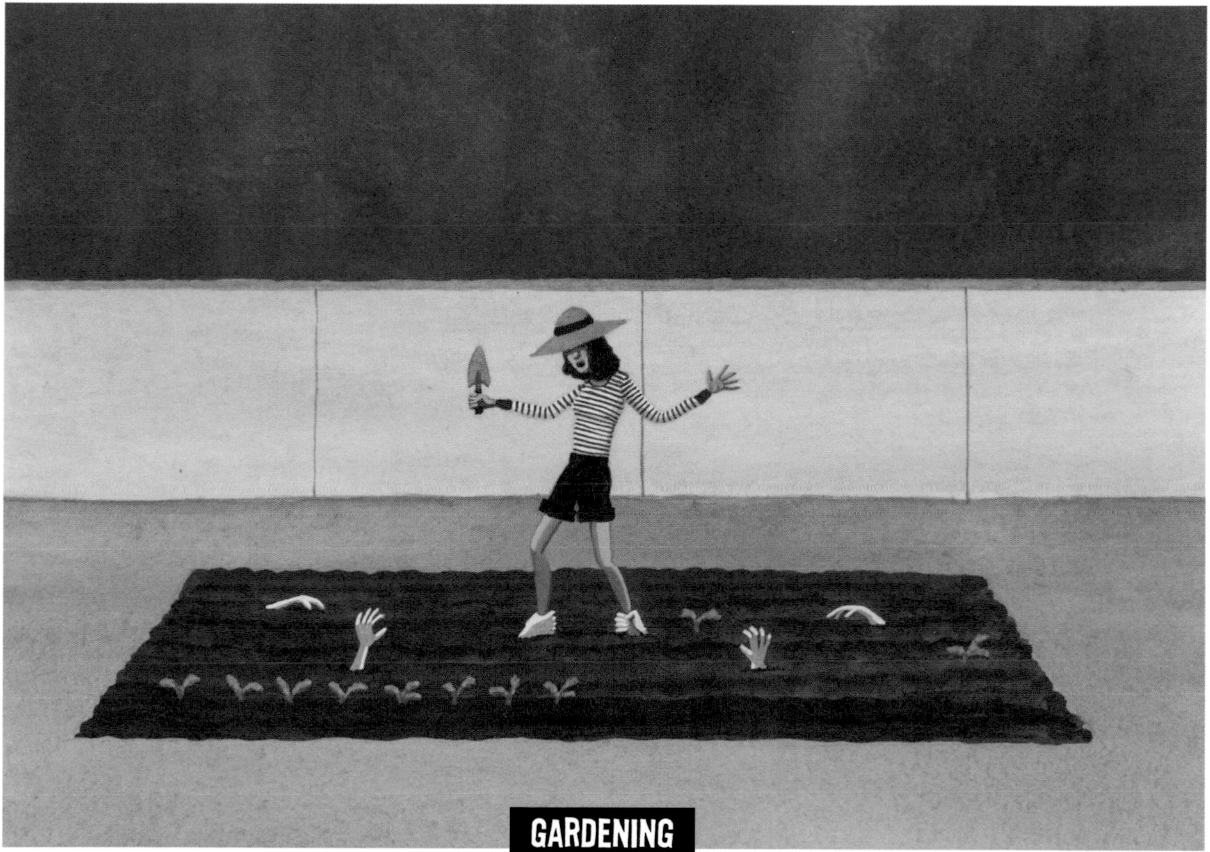

GARDENING

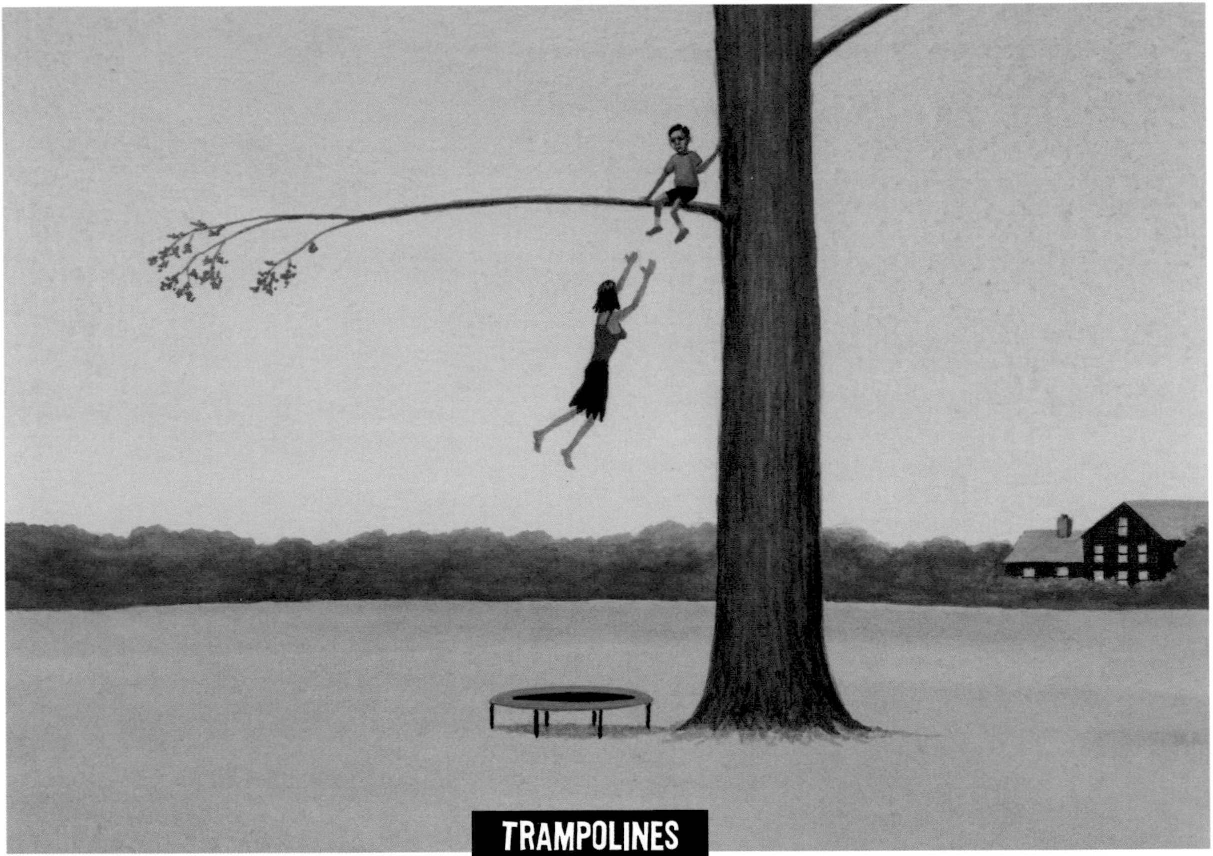

TRAMPOLINES

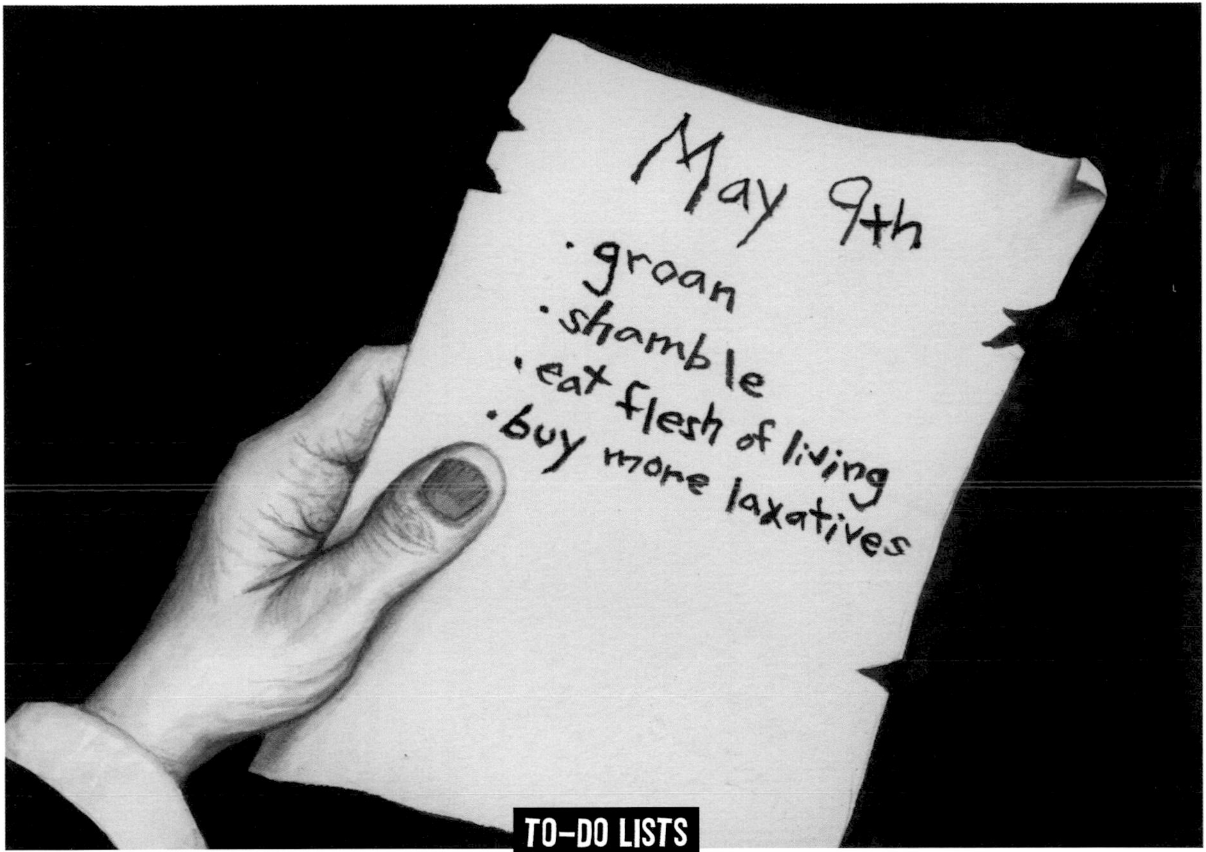
May 9th
·groan
·shamble
·eat flesh of living
·buy more laxatives

TO-DO LISTS

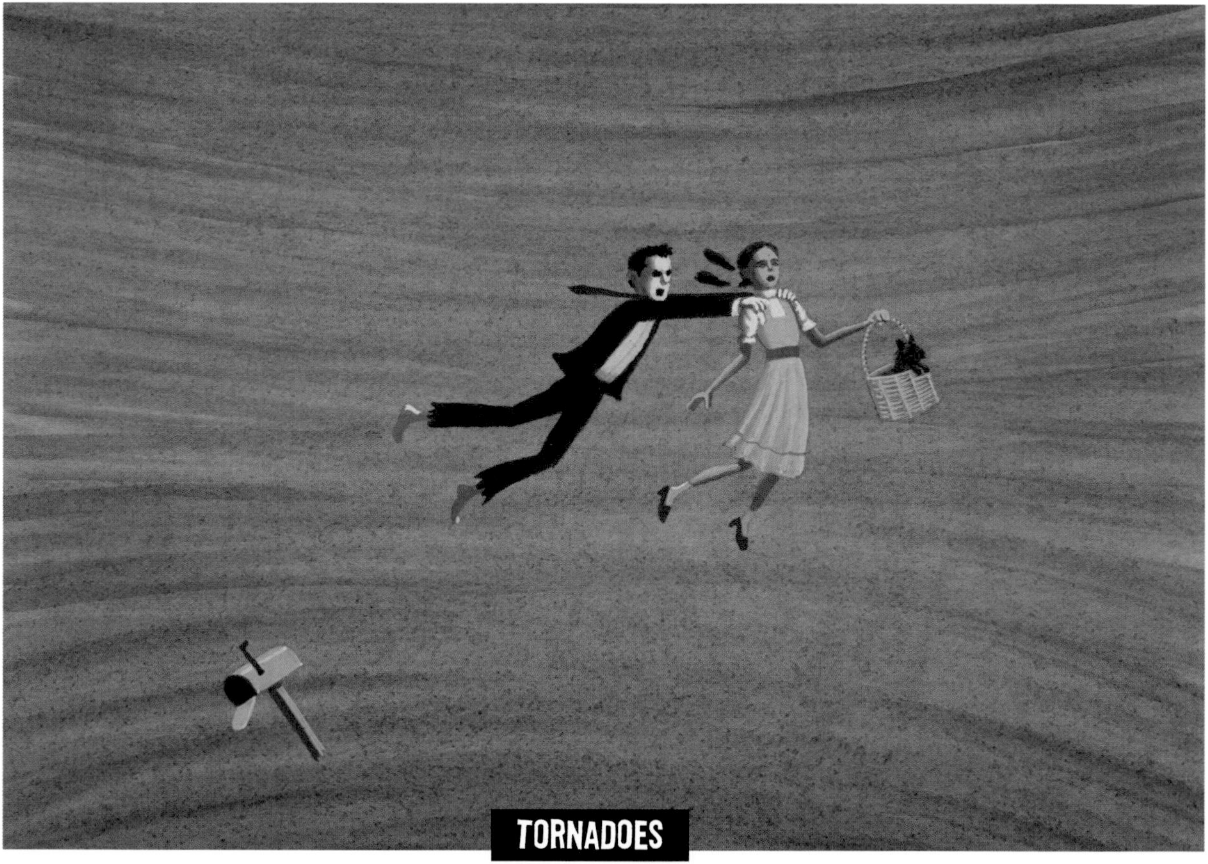

TORNADOES

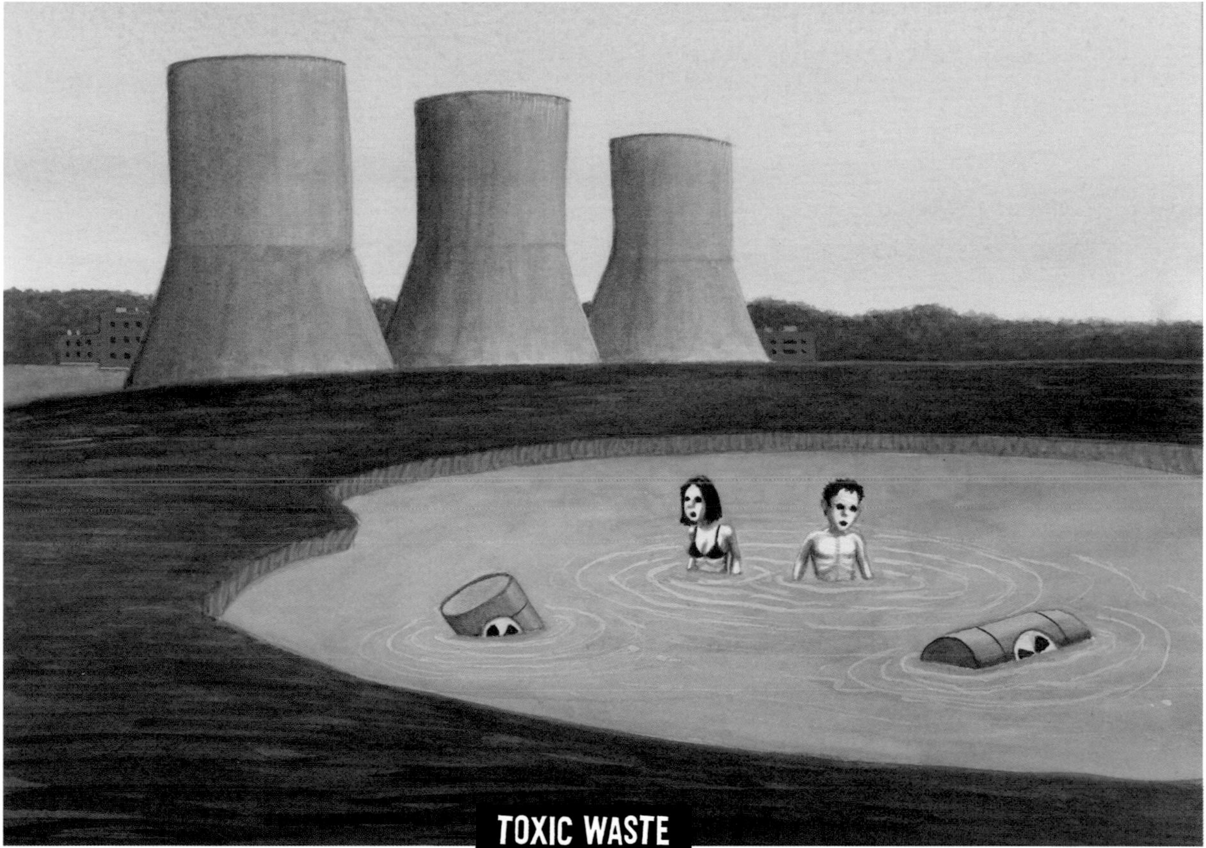

TOXIC WASTE

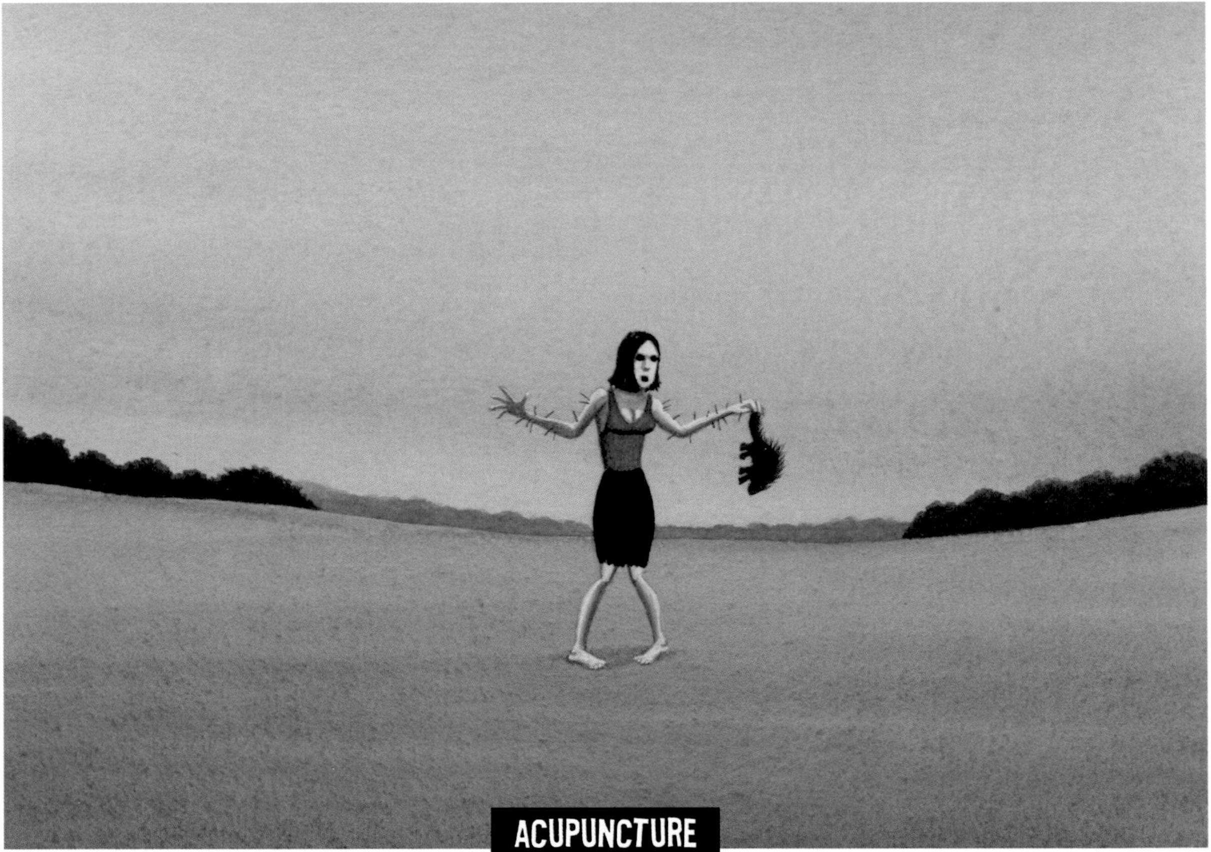

ACUPUNCTURE

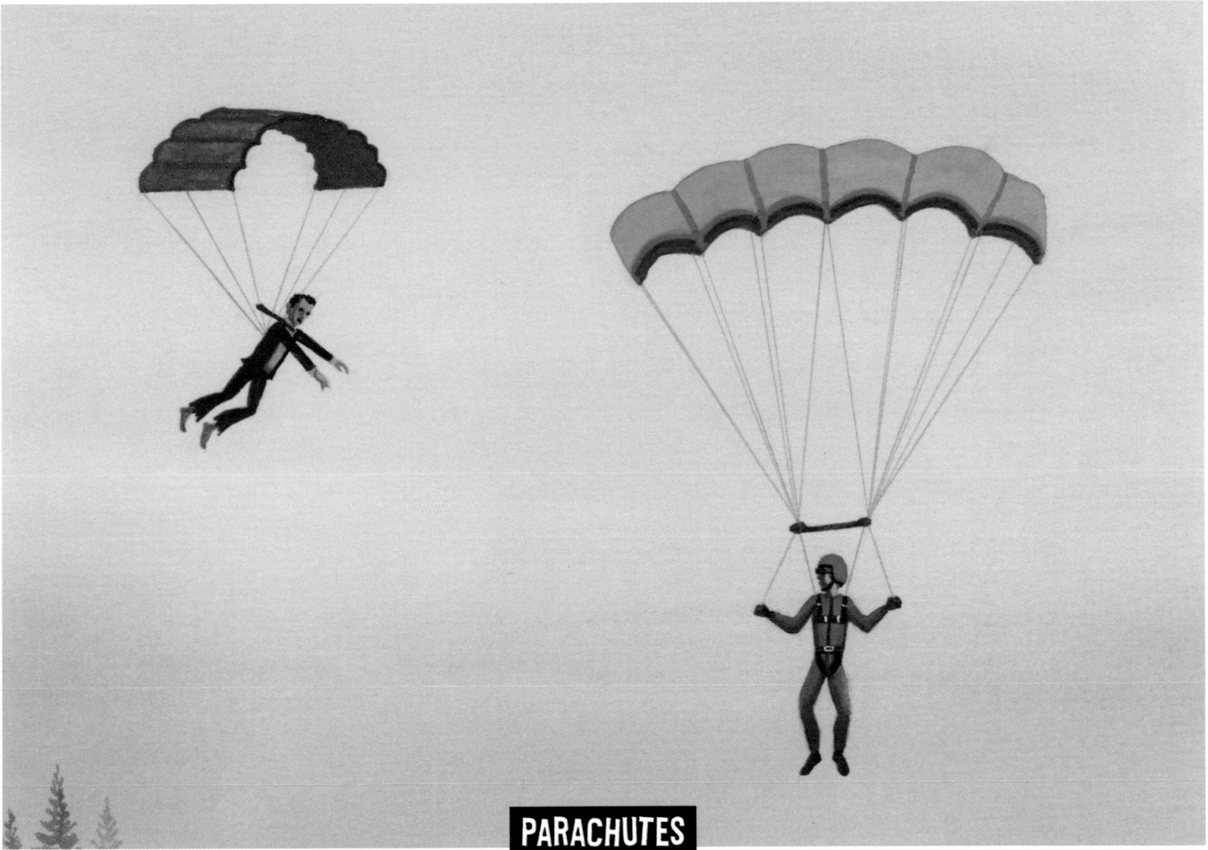

PARACHUTES

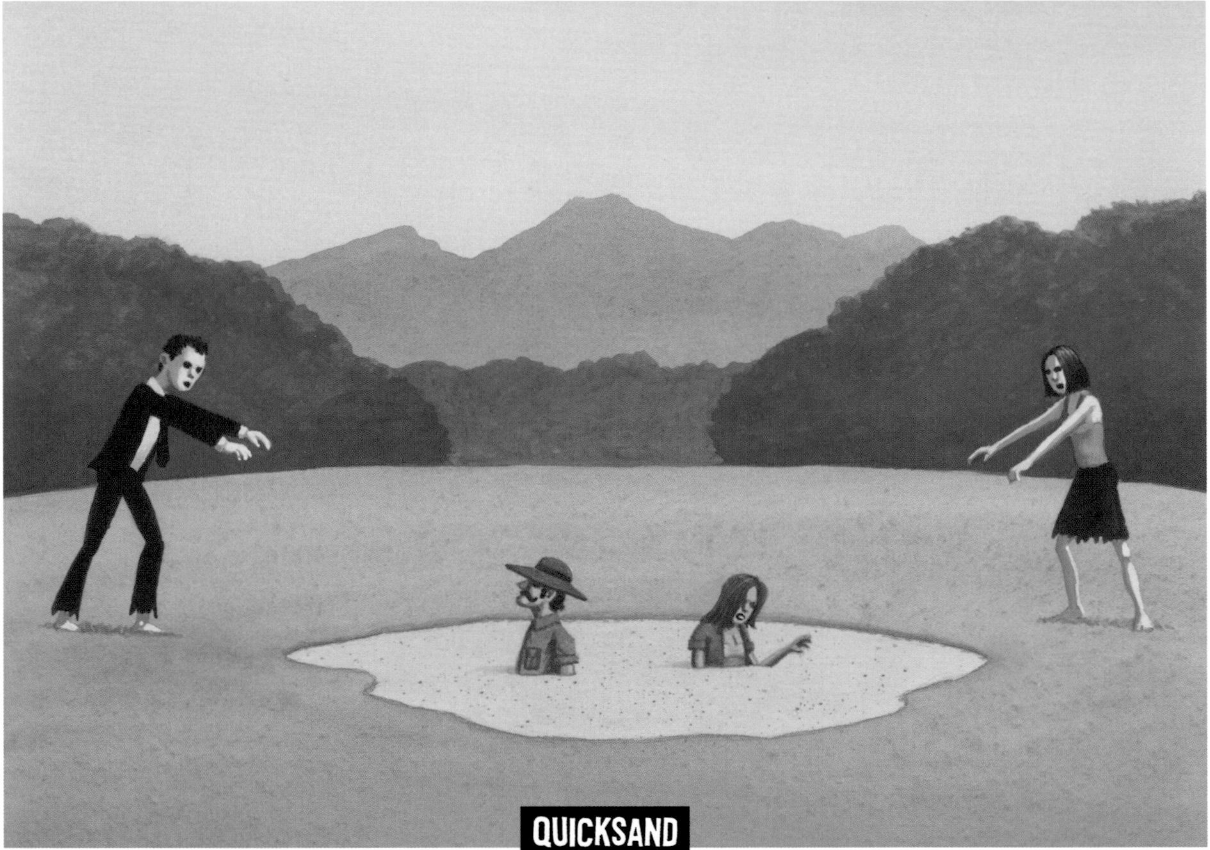

QUICKSAND

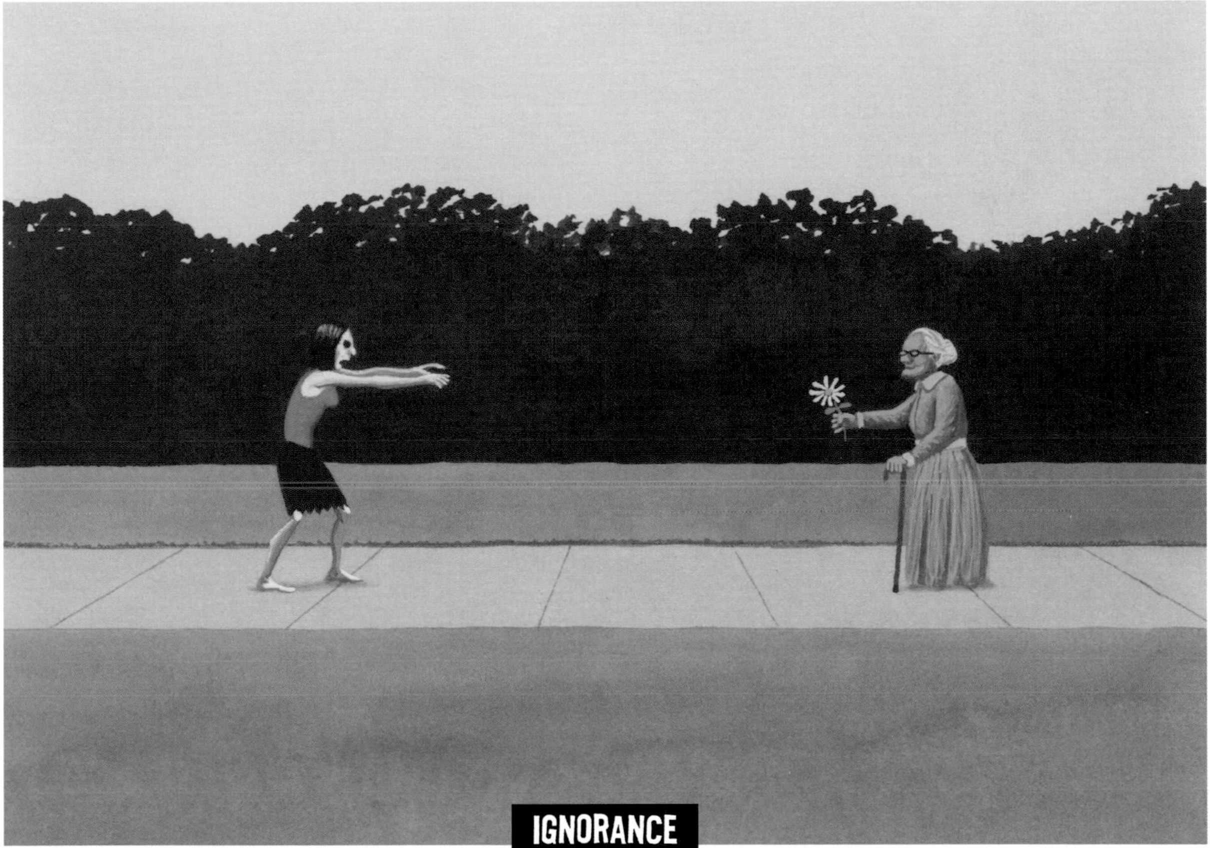

IGNORANCE

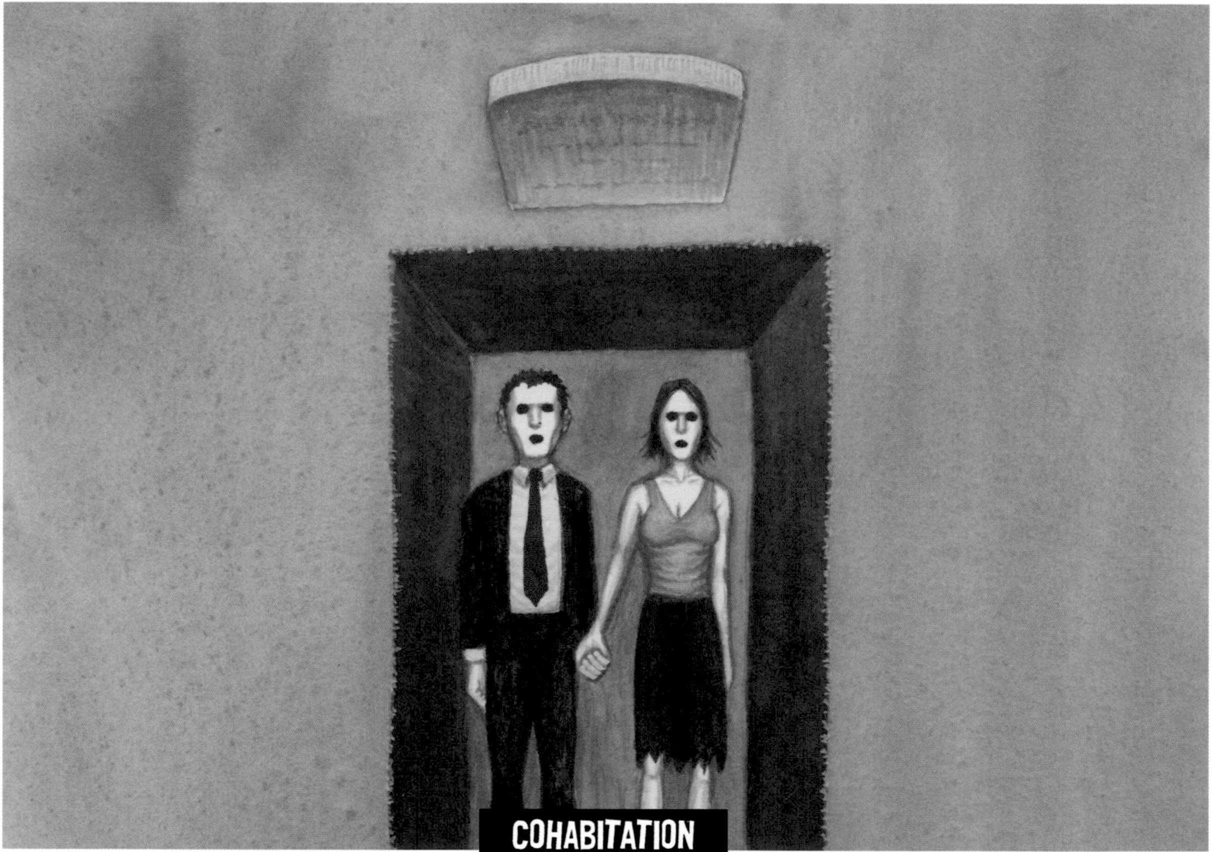

COHABITATION

ZOMBIES HAVE MAJOR ISSUES WITH . . .

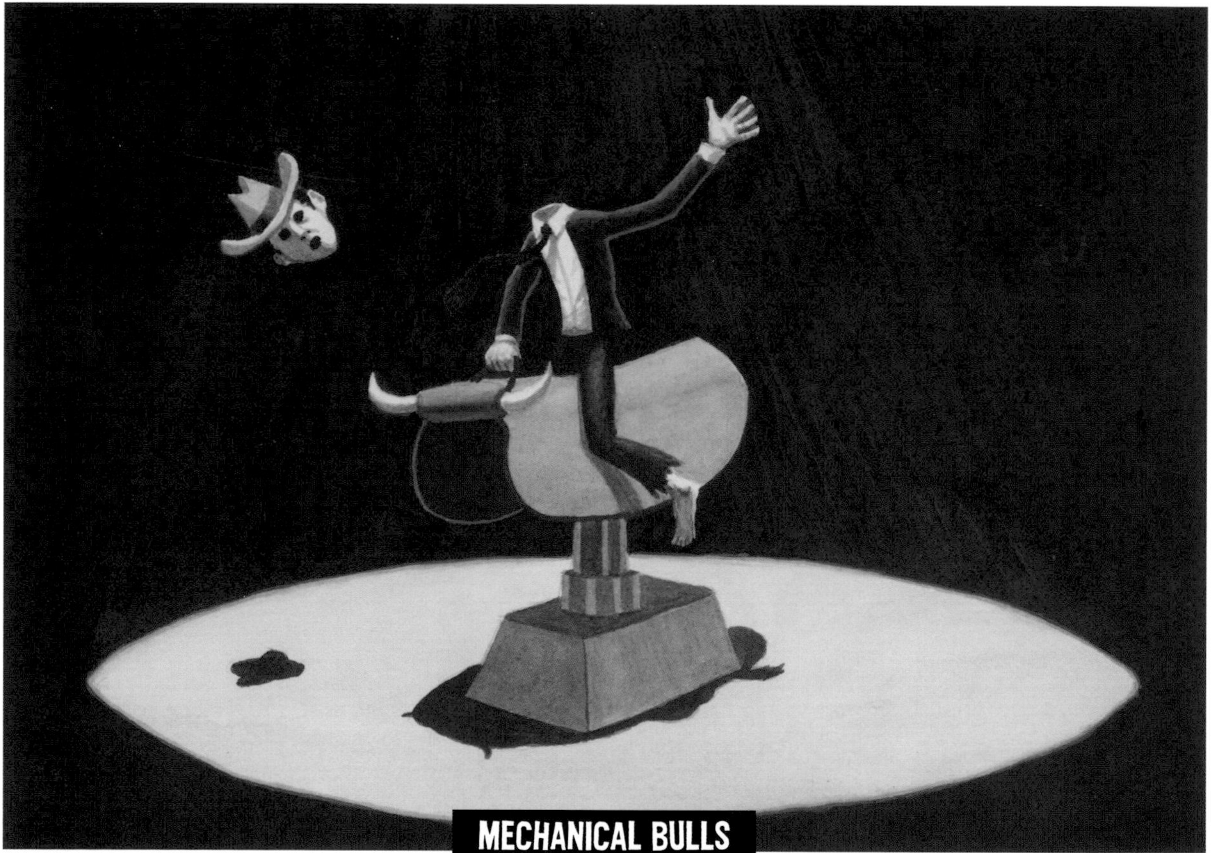

MECHANICAL BULLS

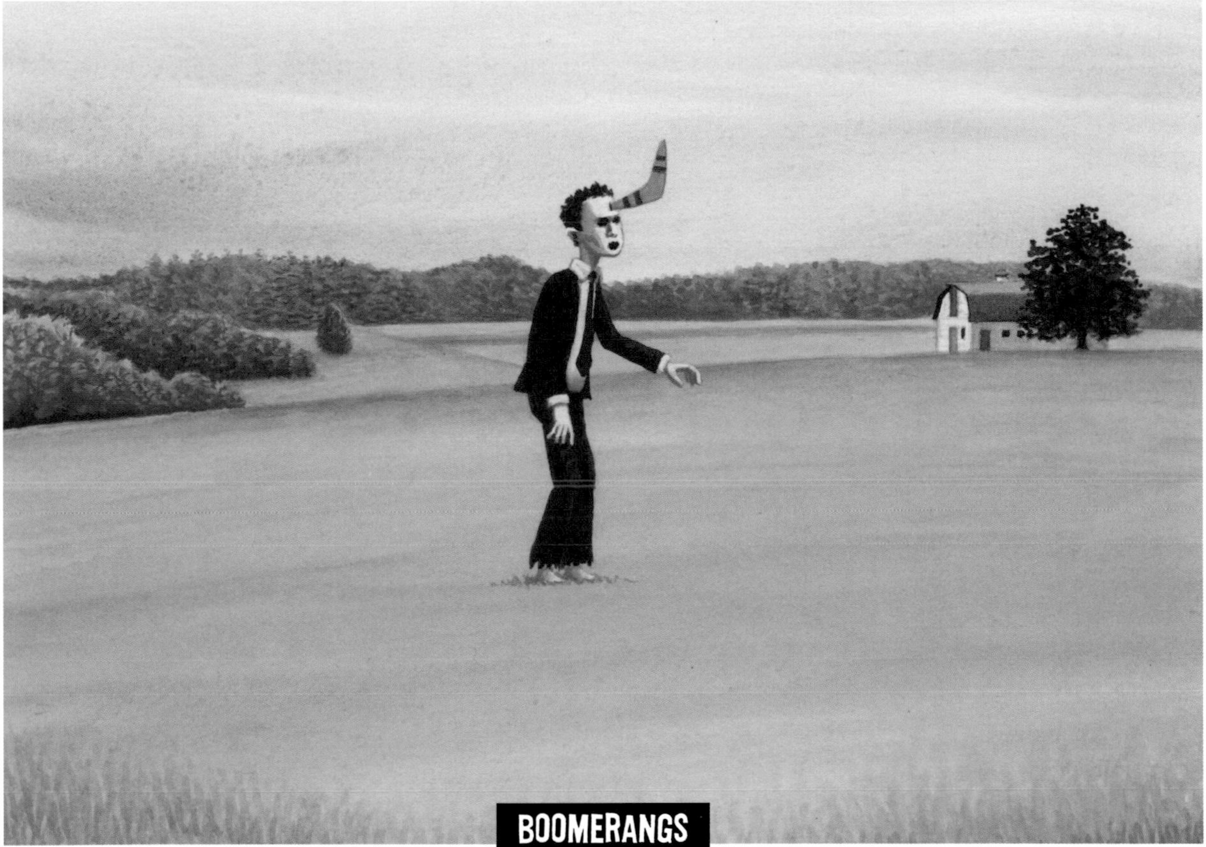

BOOMERANGS

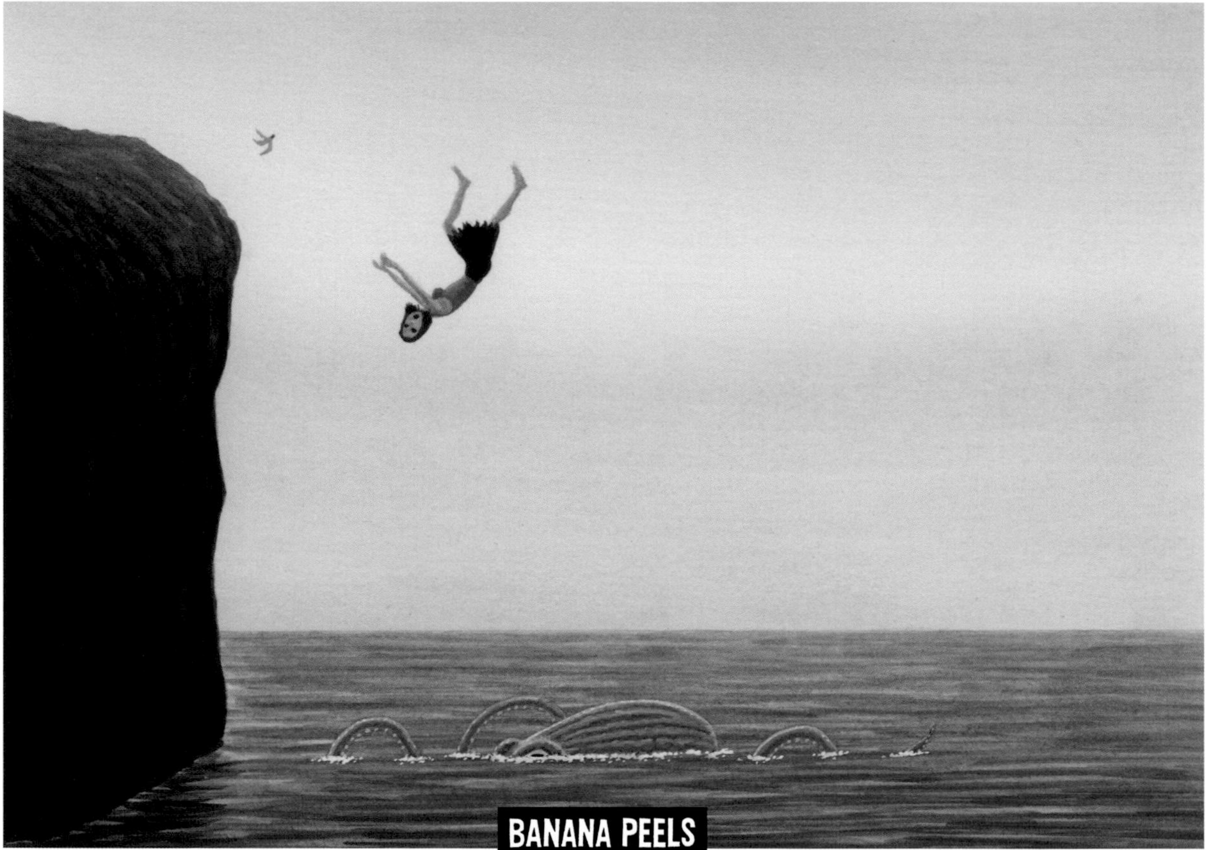

BANANA PEELS

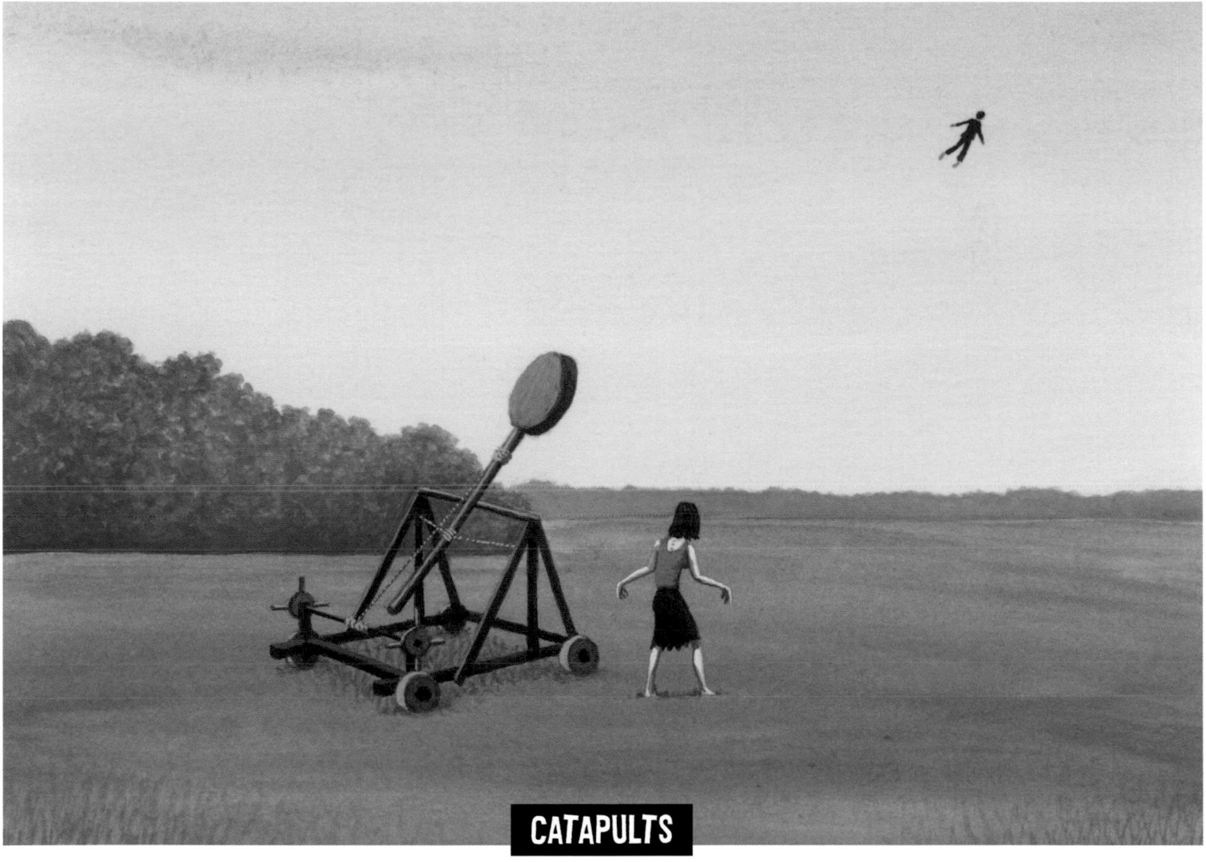

CATAPULTS

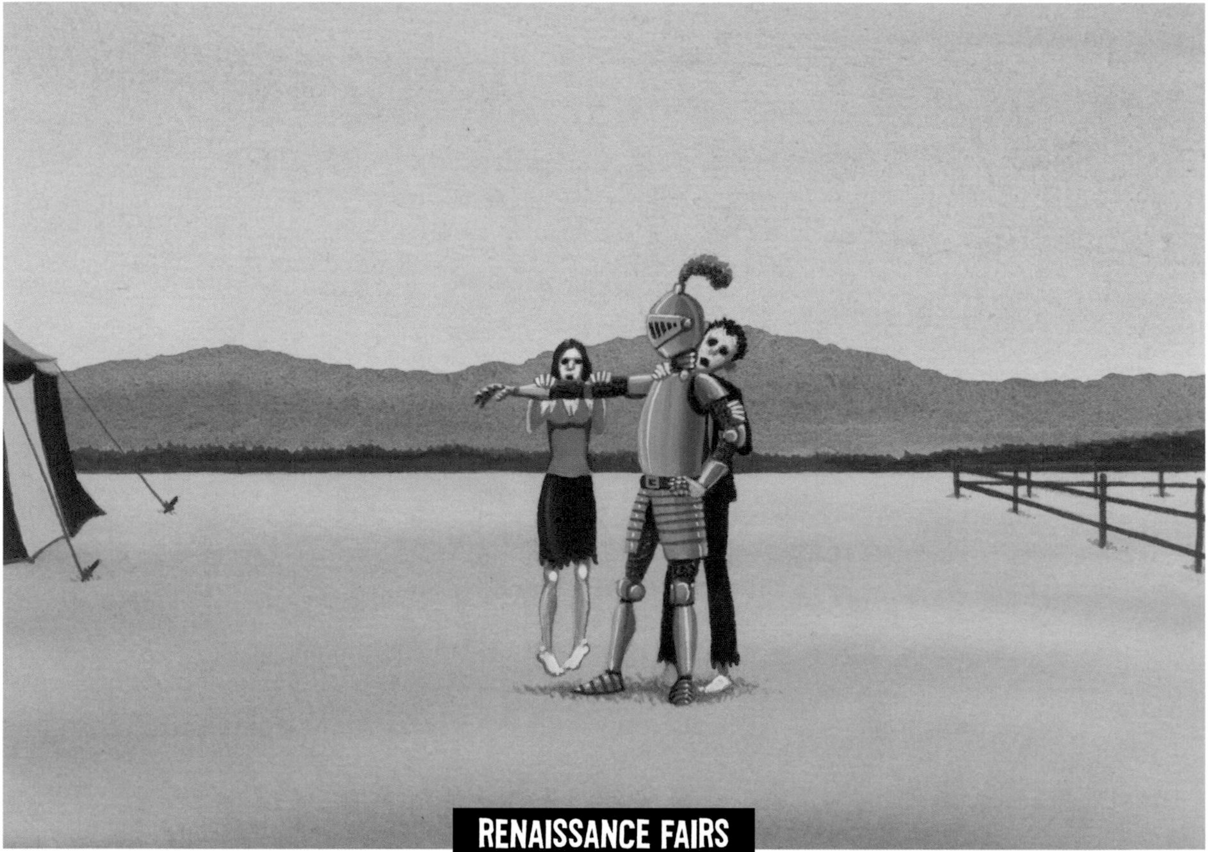

RENAISSANCE FAIRS

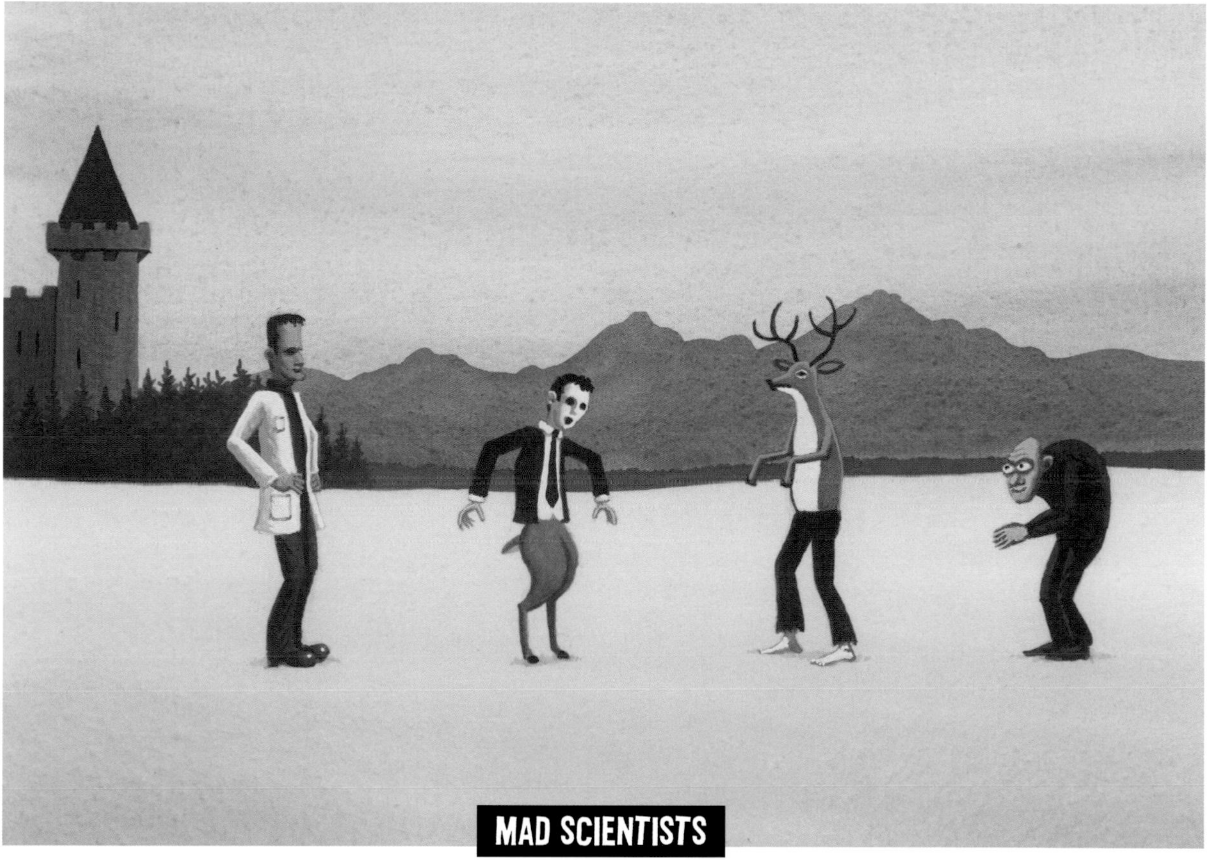
MAD SCIENTISTS

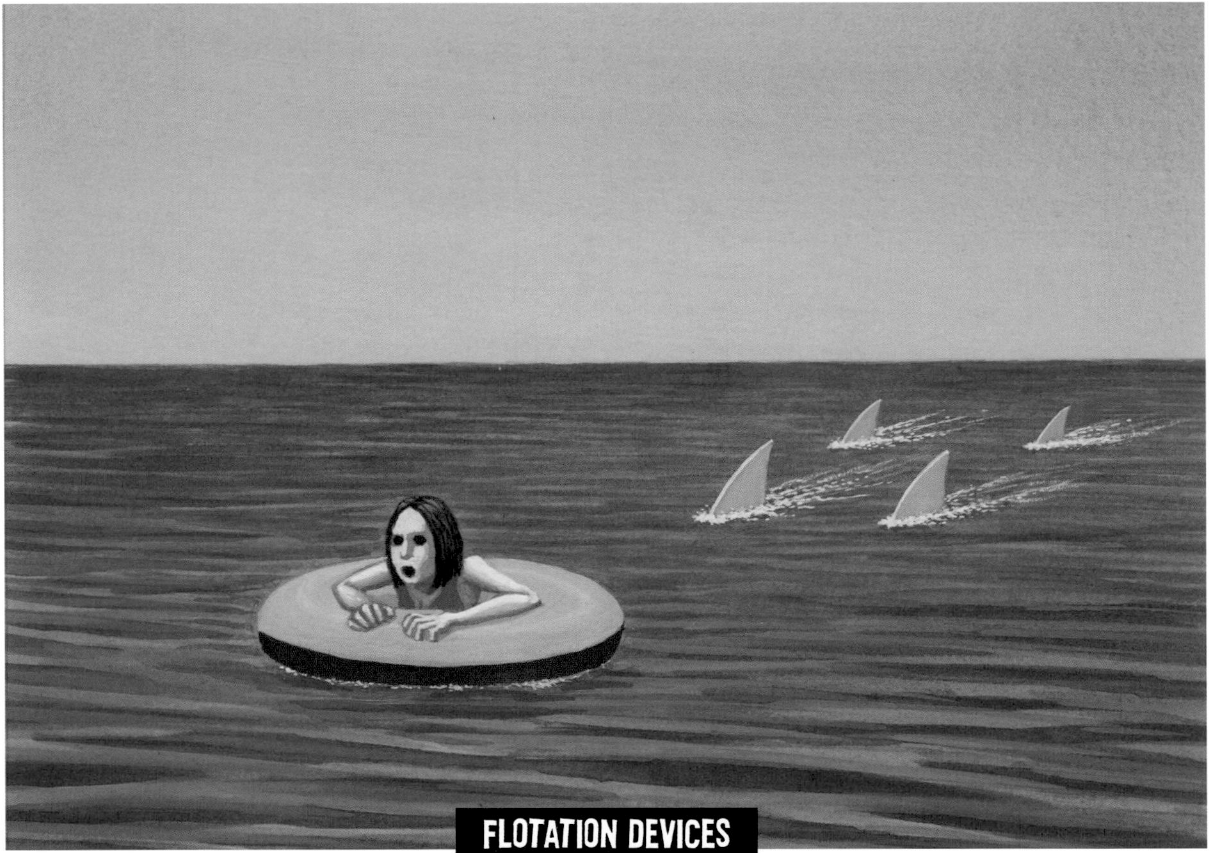

FLOTATION DEVICES

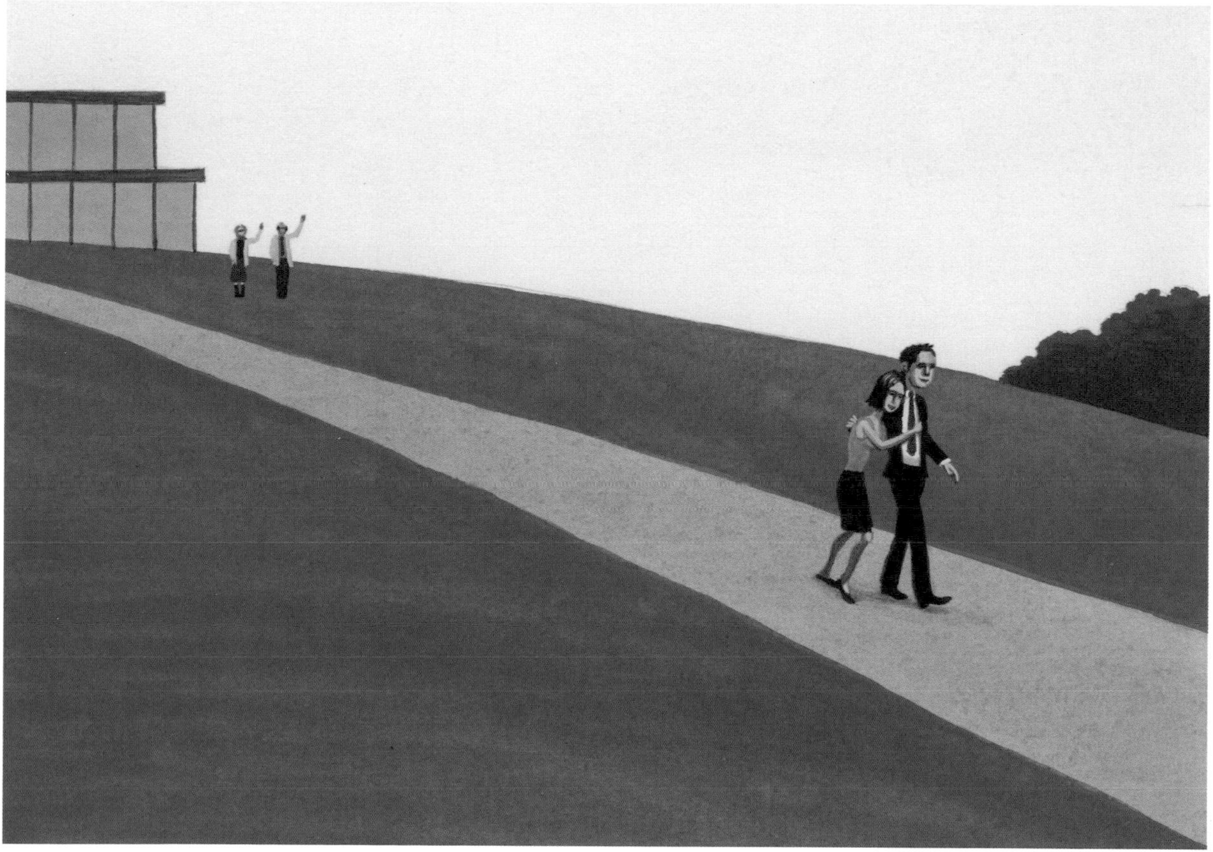

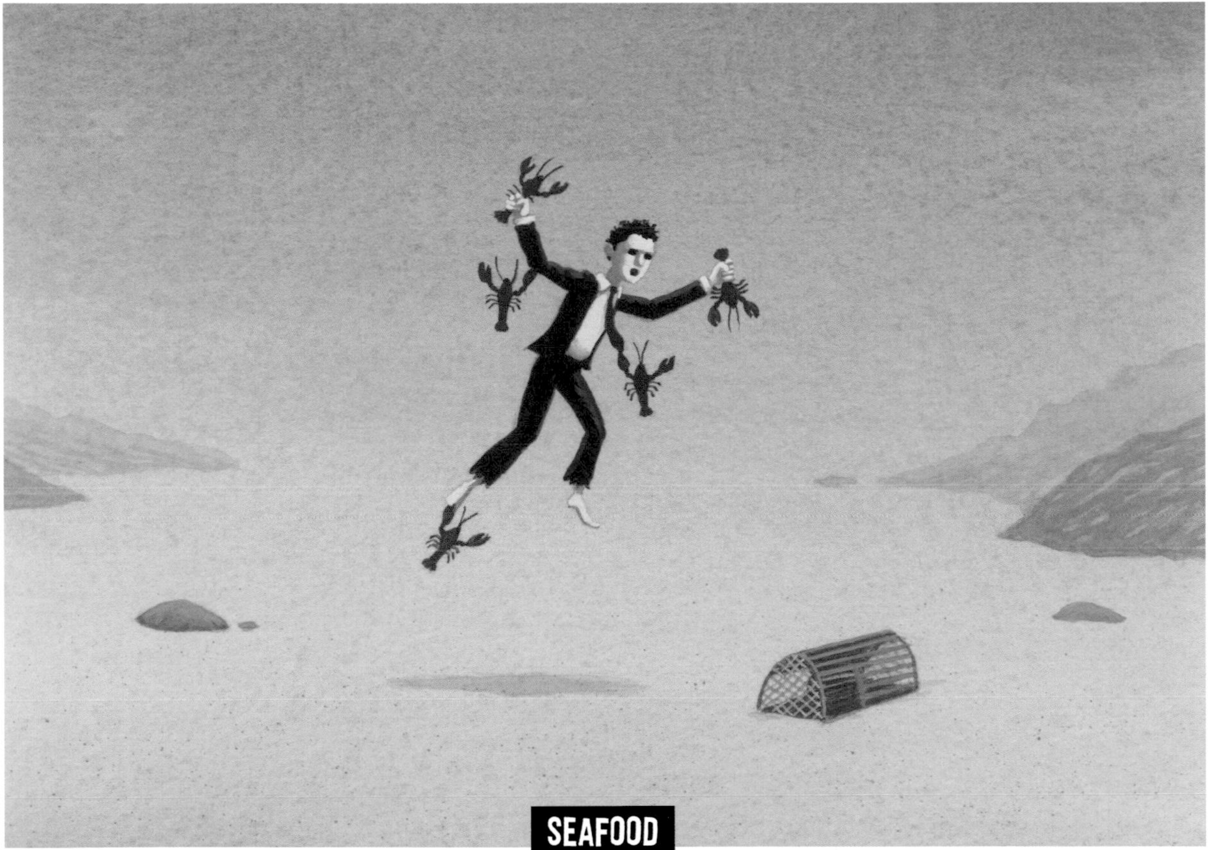

SEAFOOD

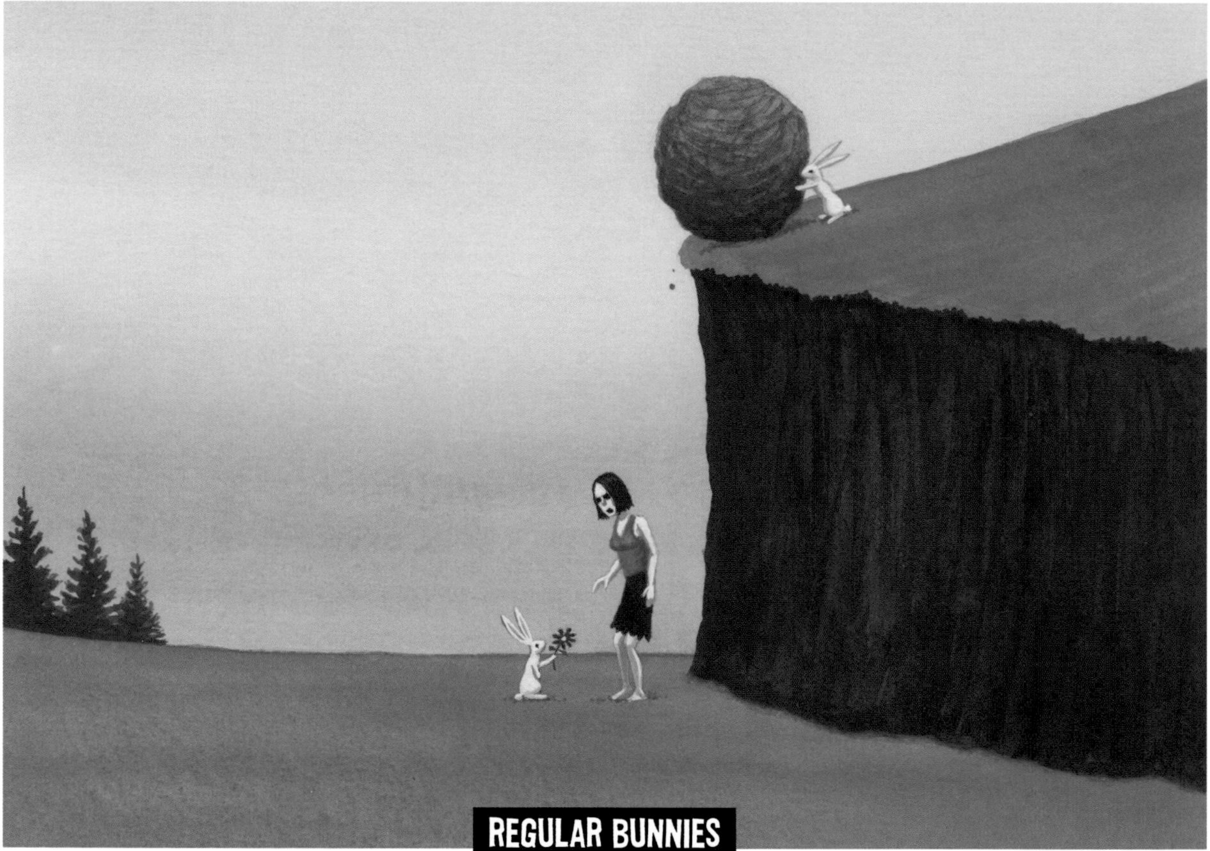

REGULAR BUNNIES

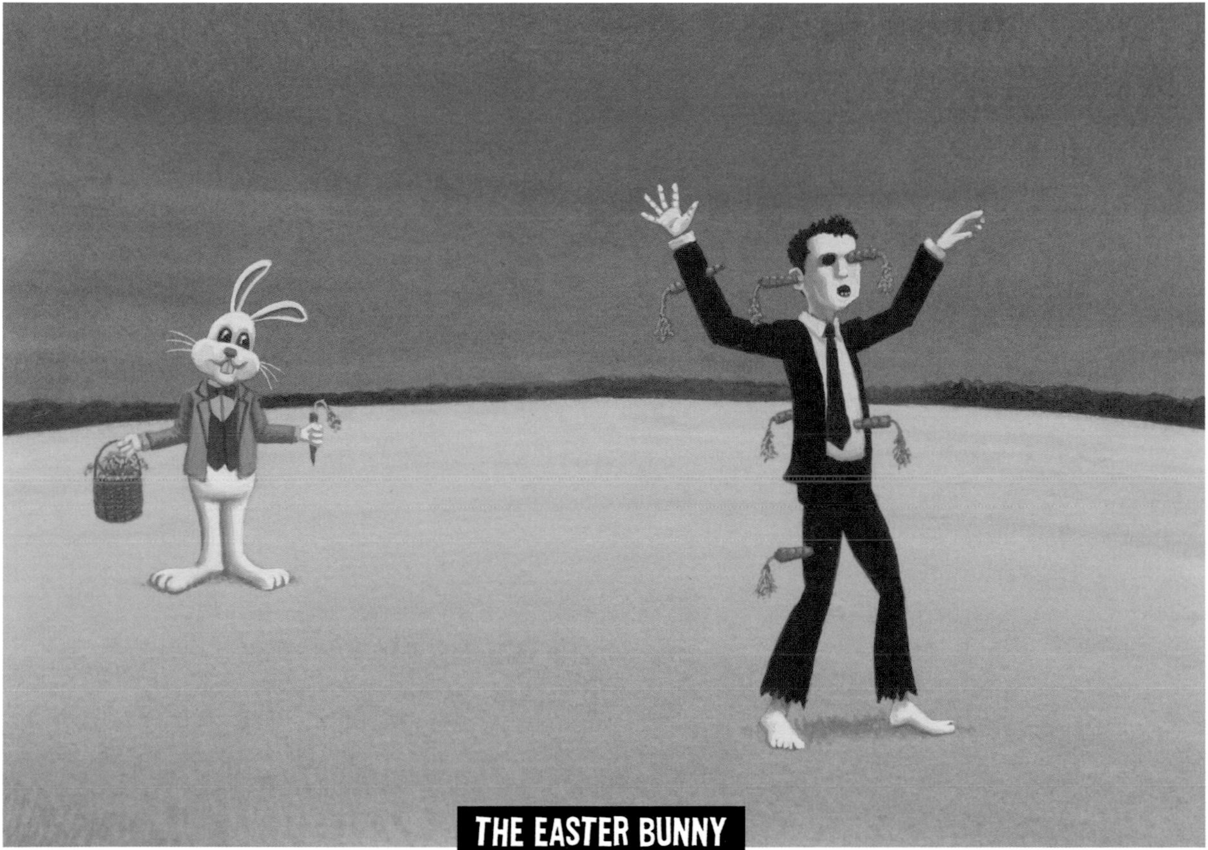

THE EASTER BUNNY

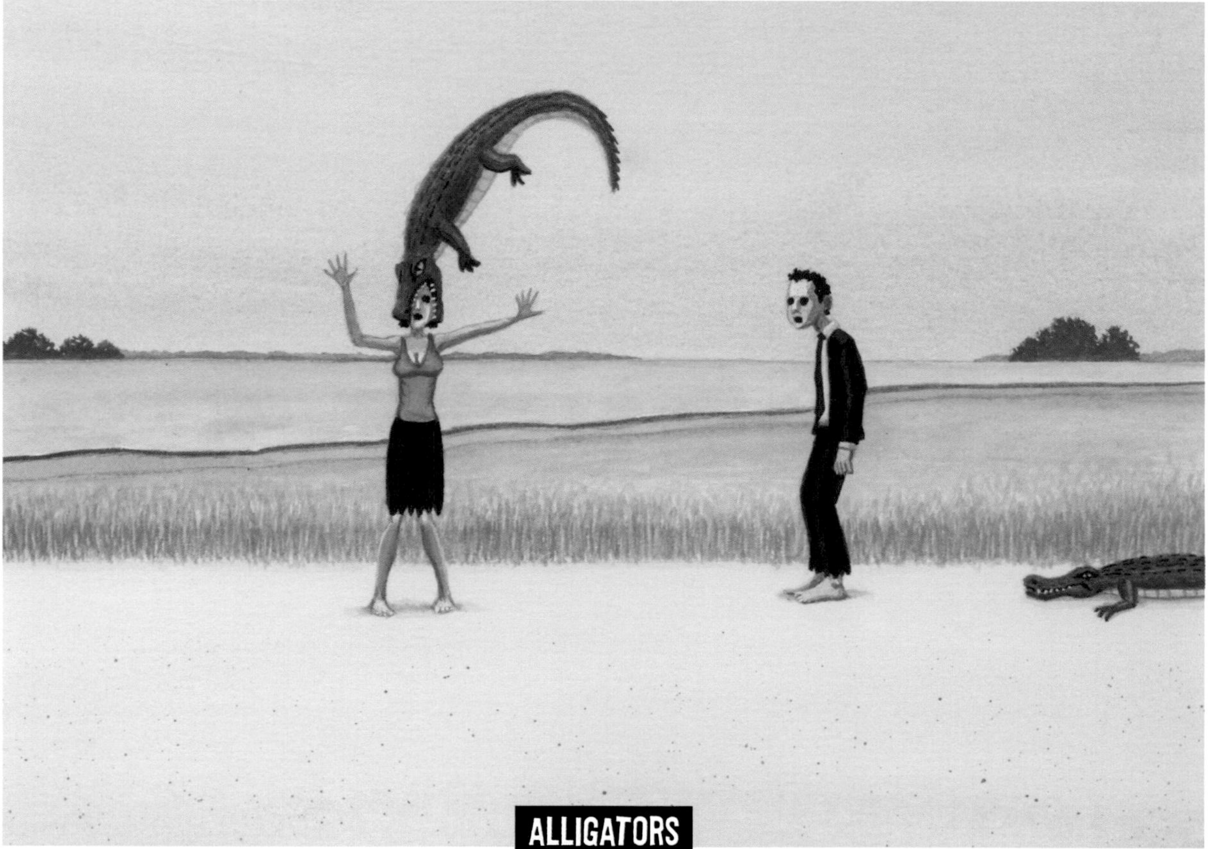

ALLIGATORS

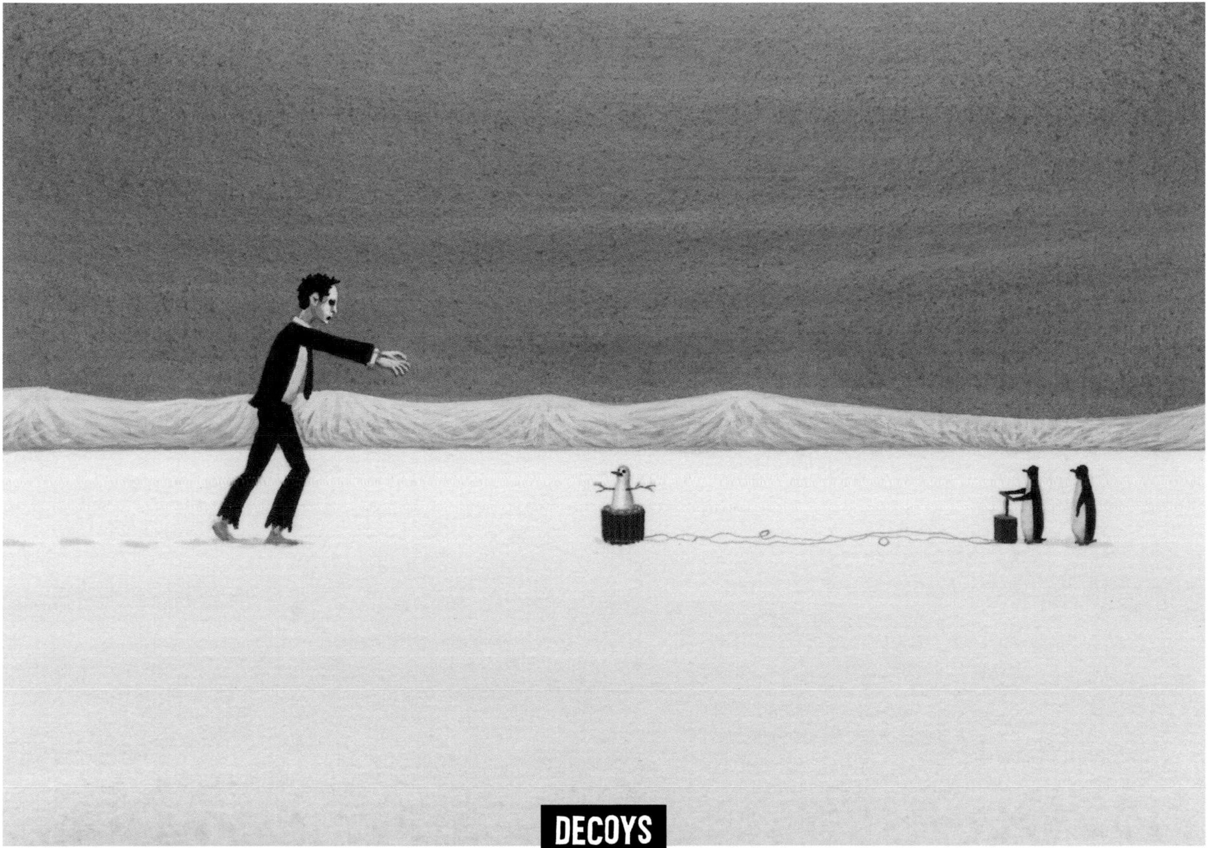

DECOYS

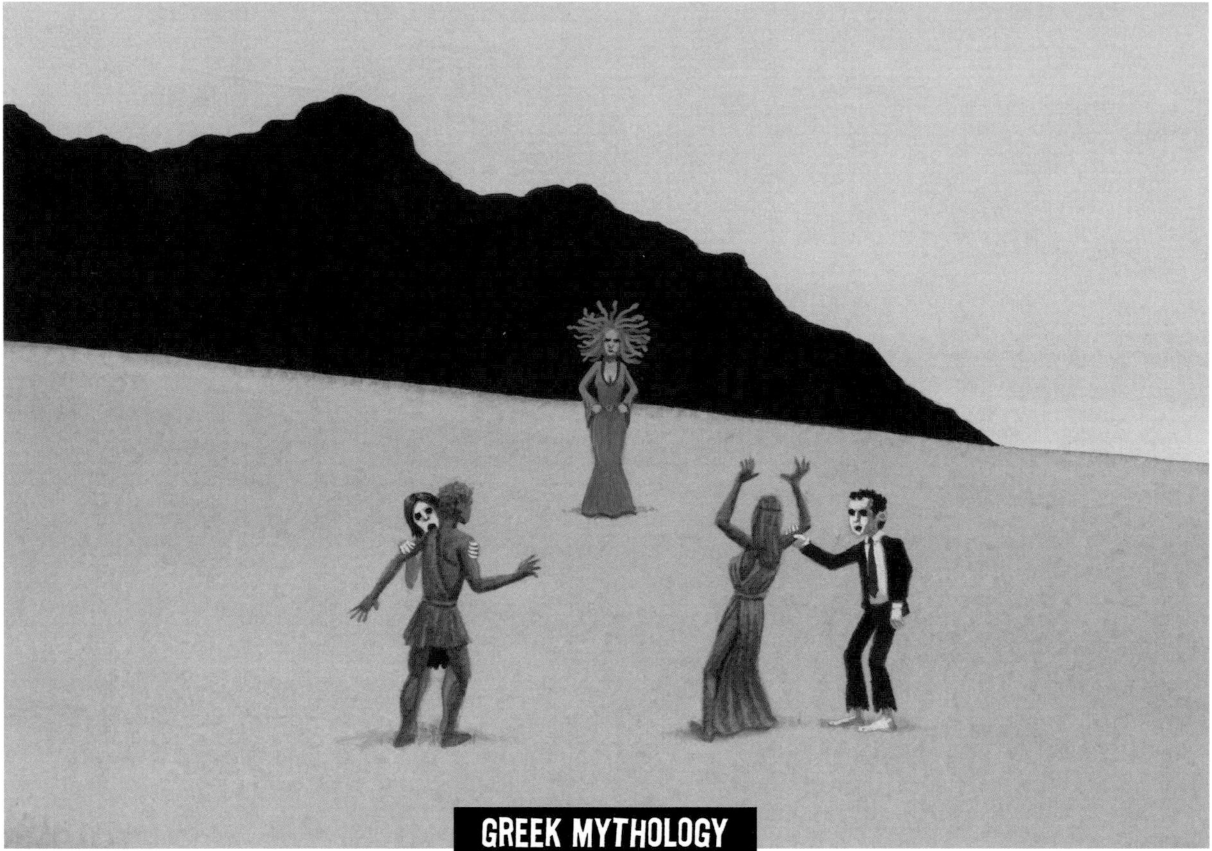

GREEK MYTHOLOGY

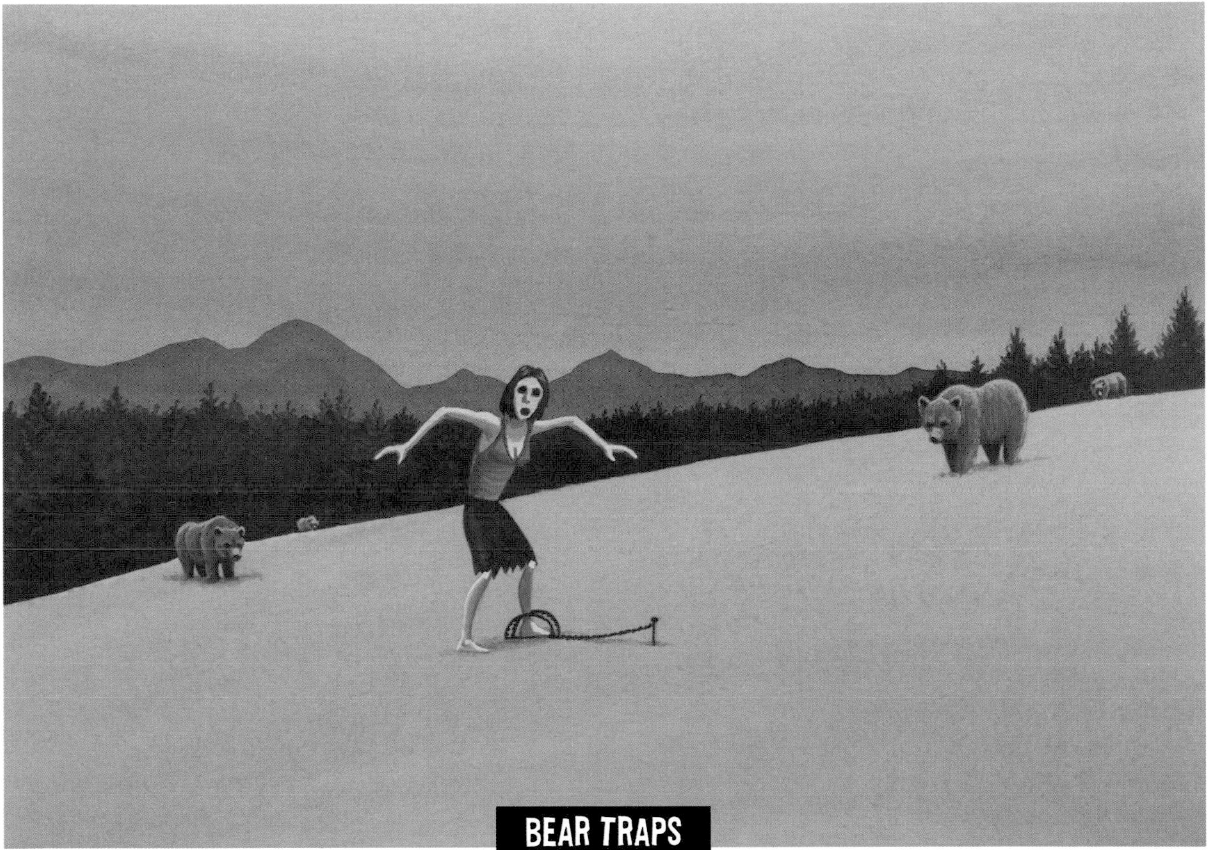

BEAR TRAPS

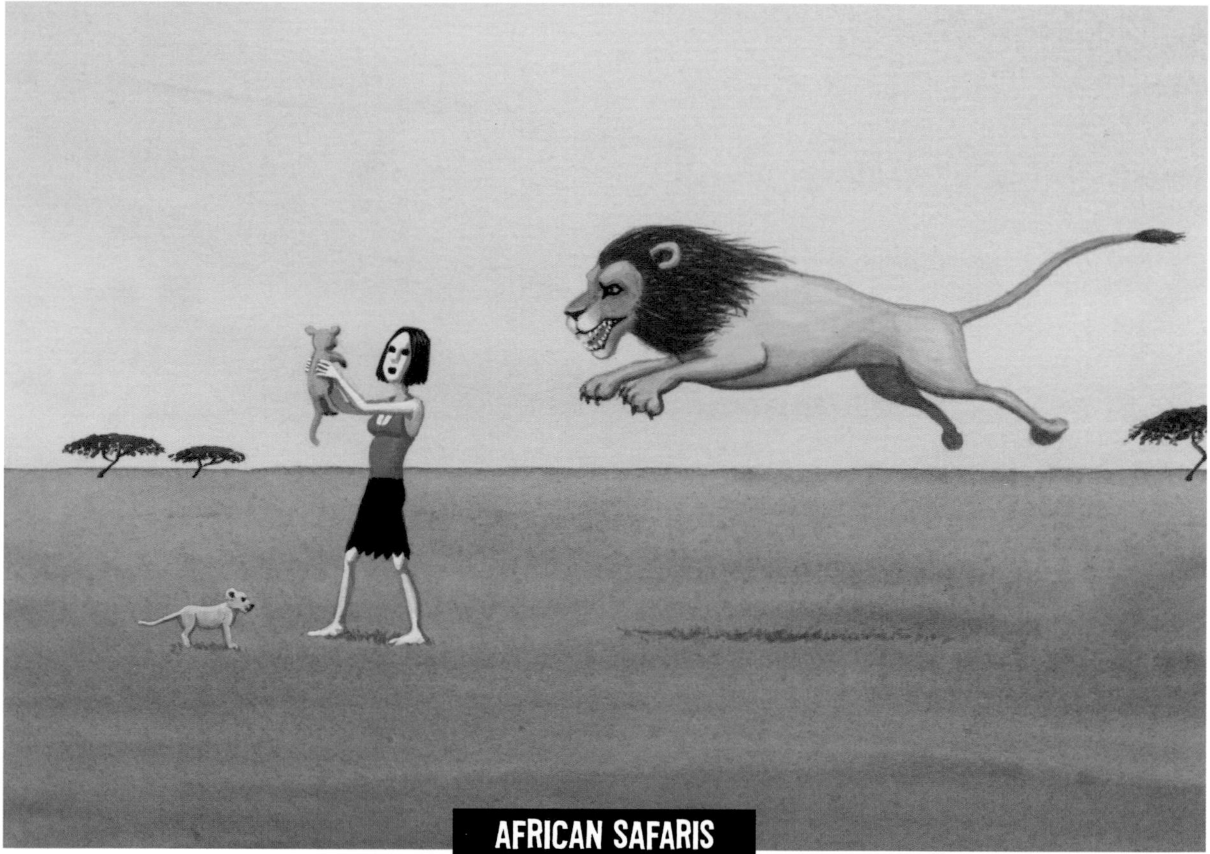

AFRICAN SAFARIS

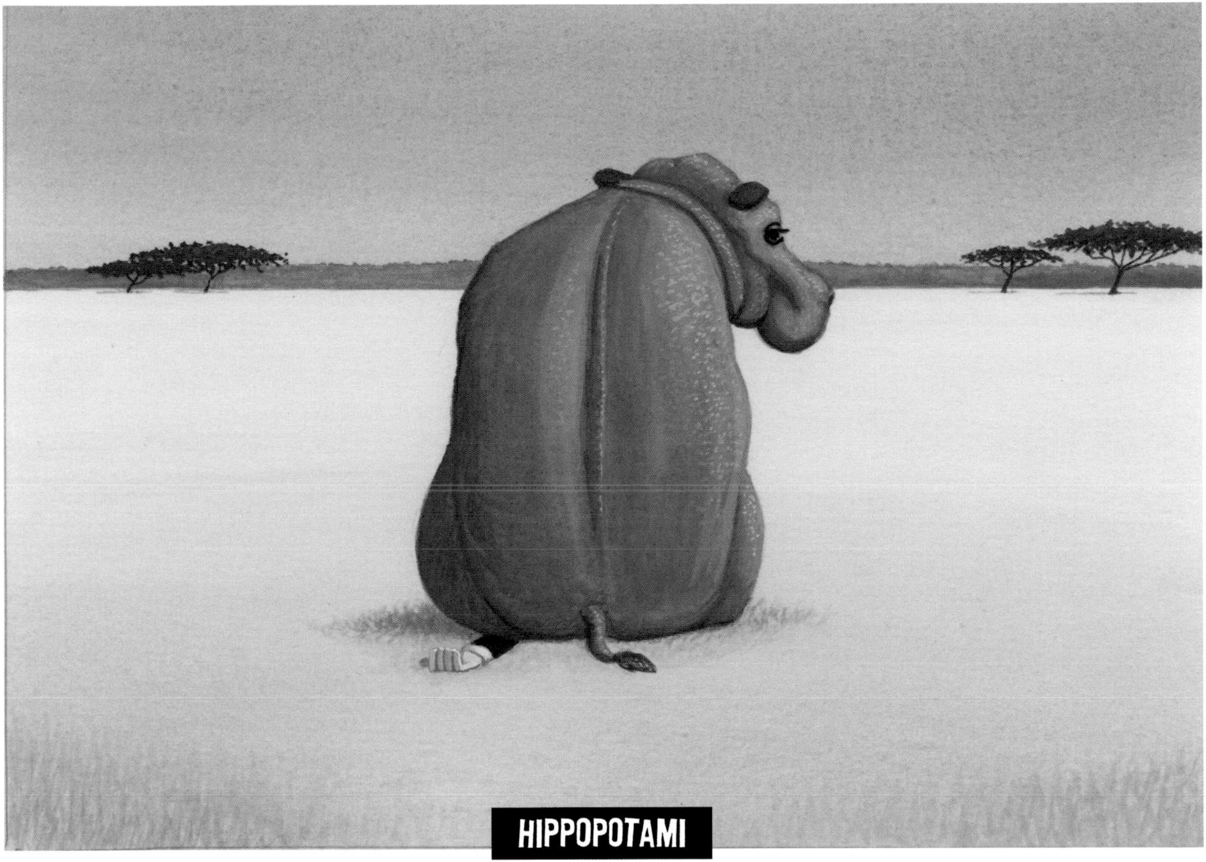

HIPPOPOTAMI

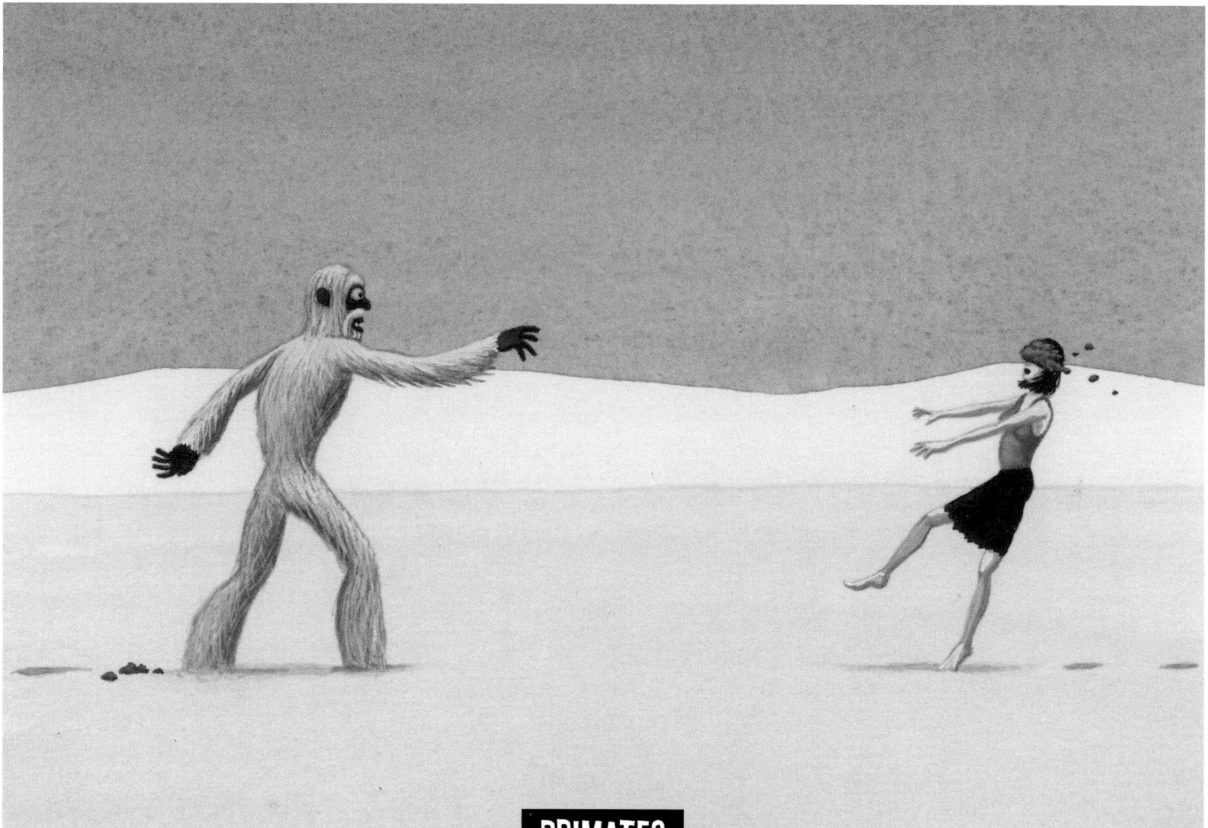

PRIMATES

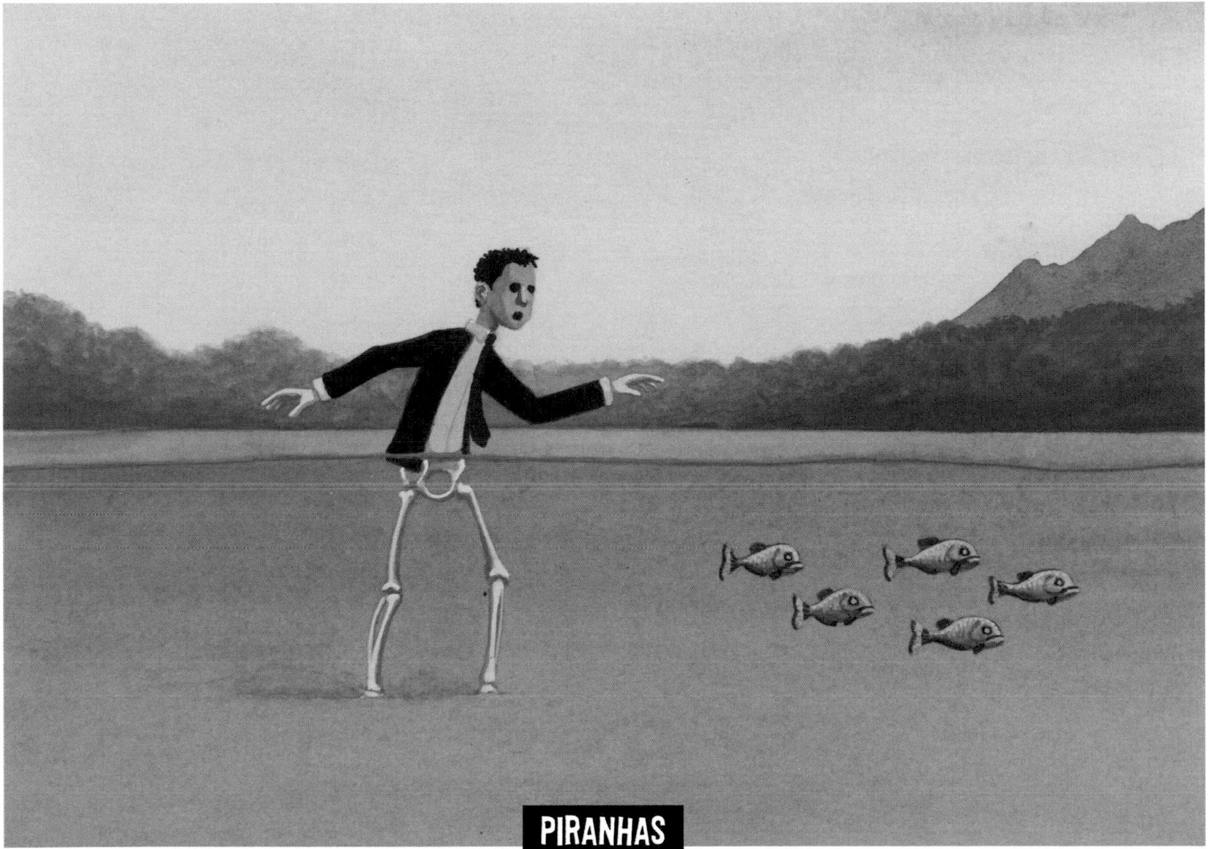

PIRANHAS

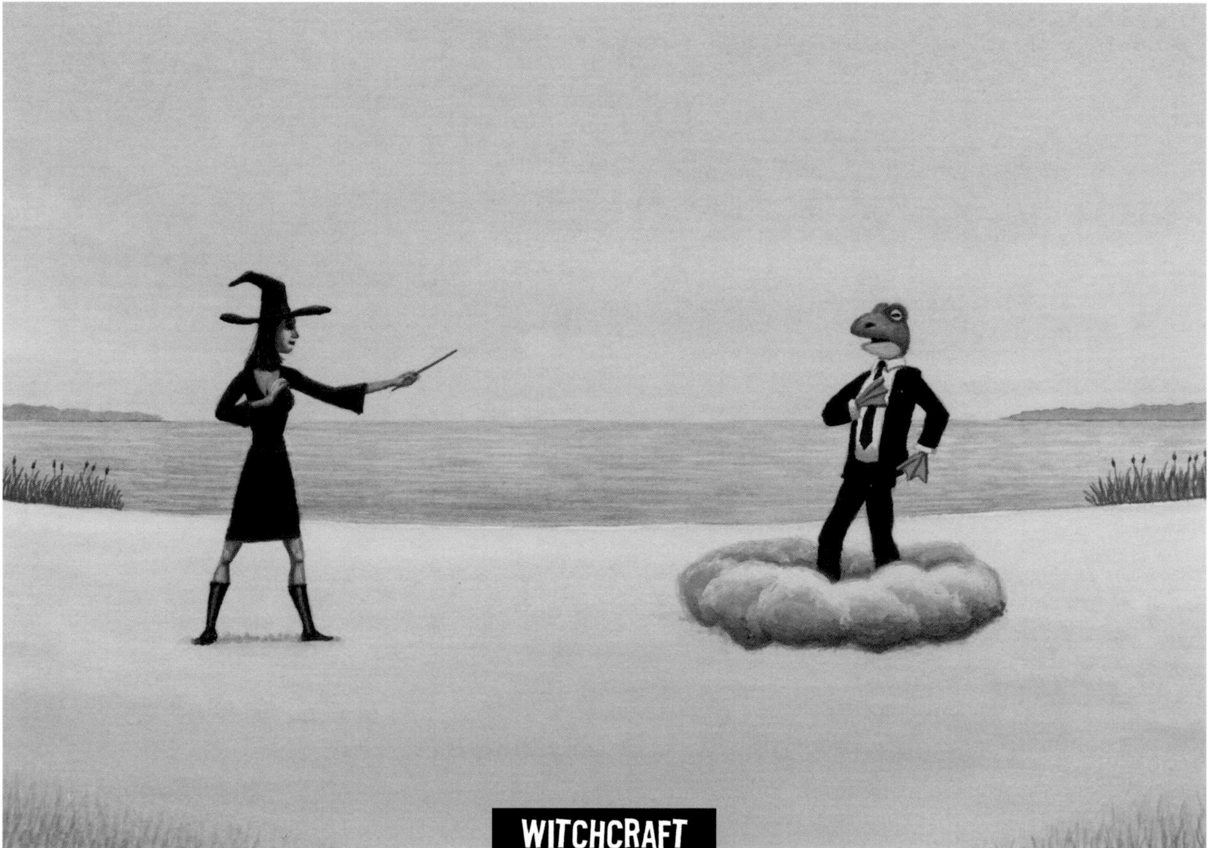

WITCHCRAFT

ZOMBIES REALLY WANT . . .

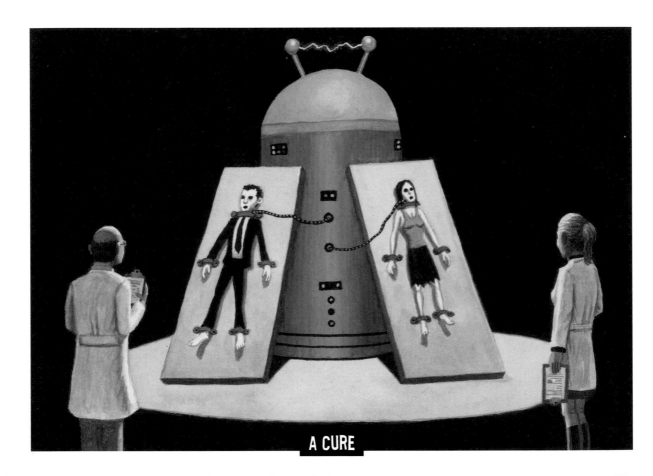

A CURE

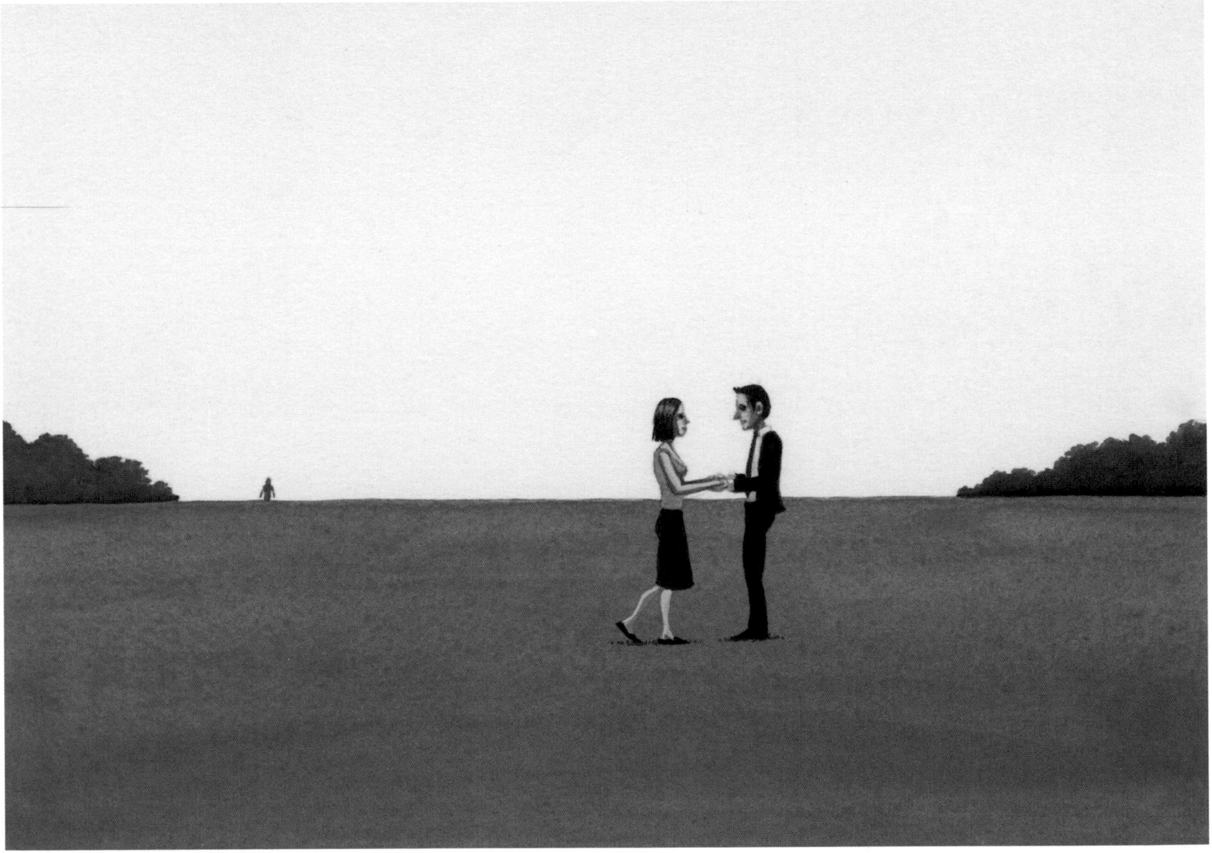

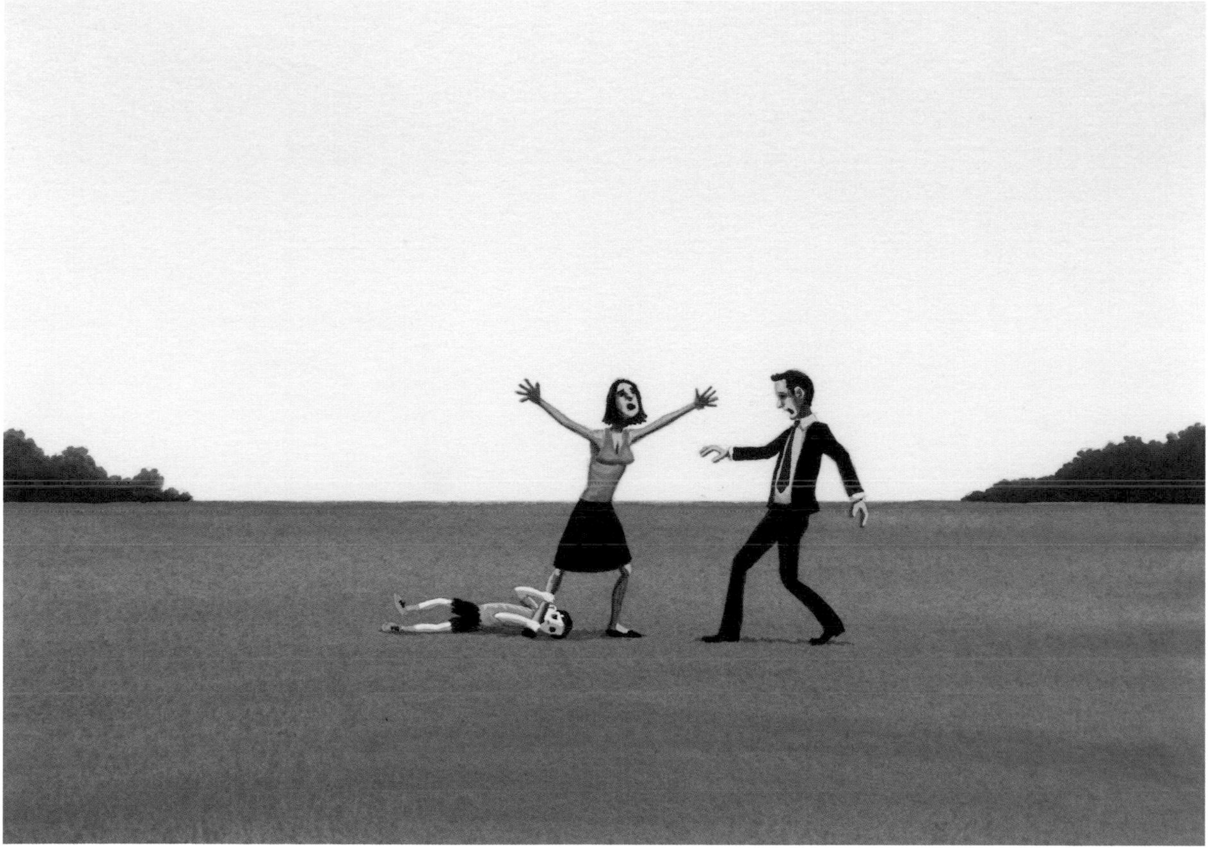

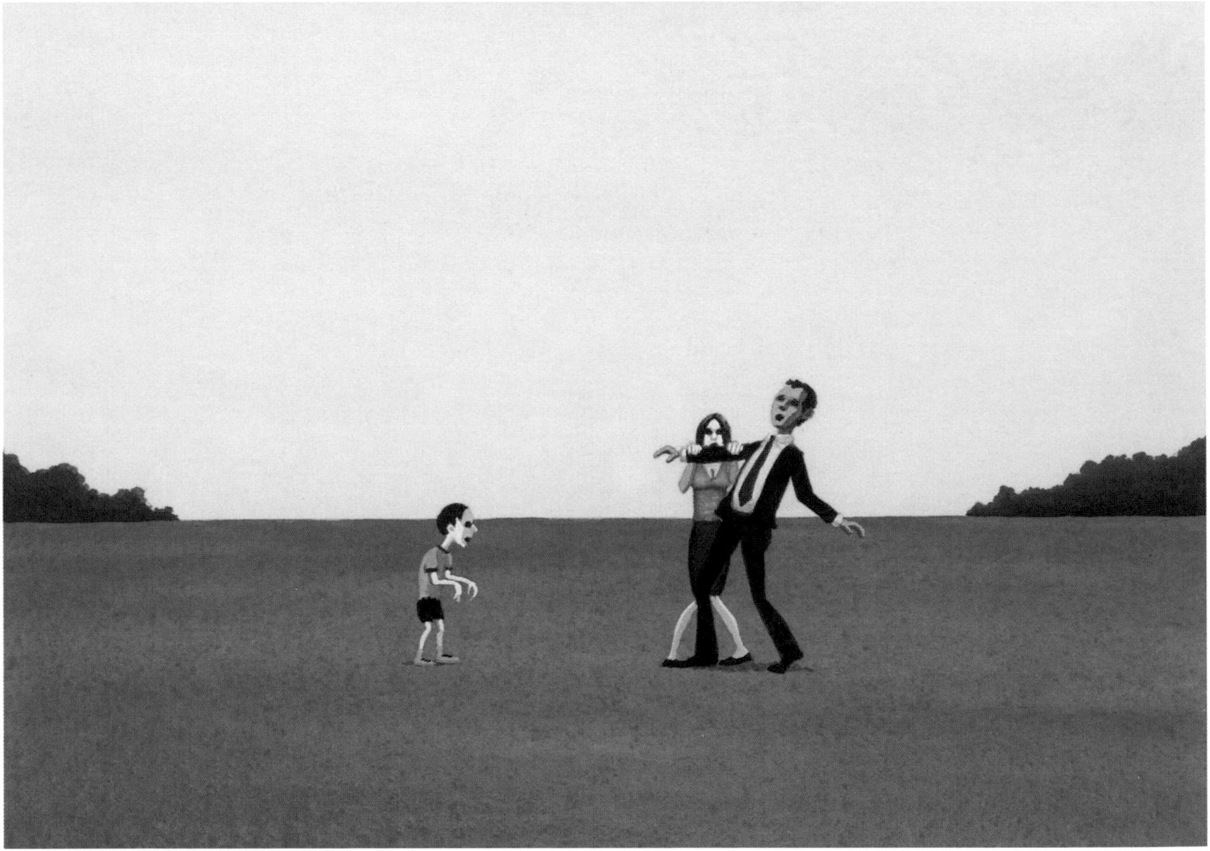

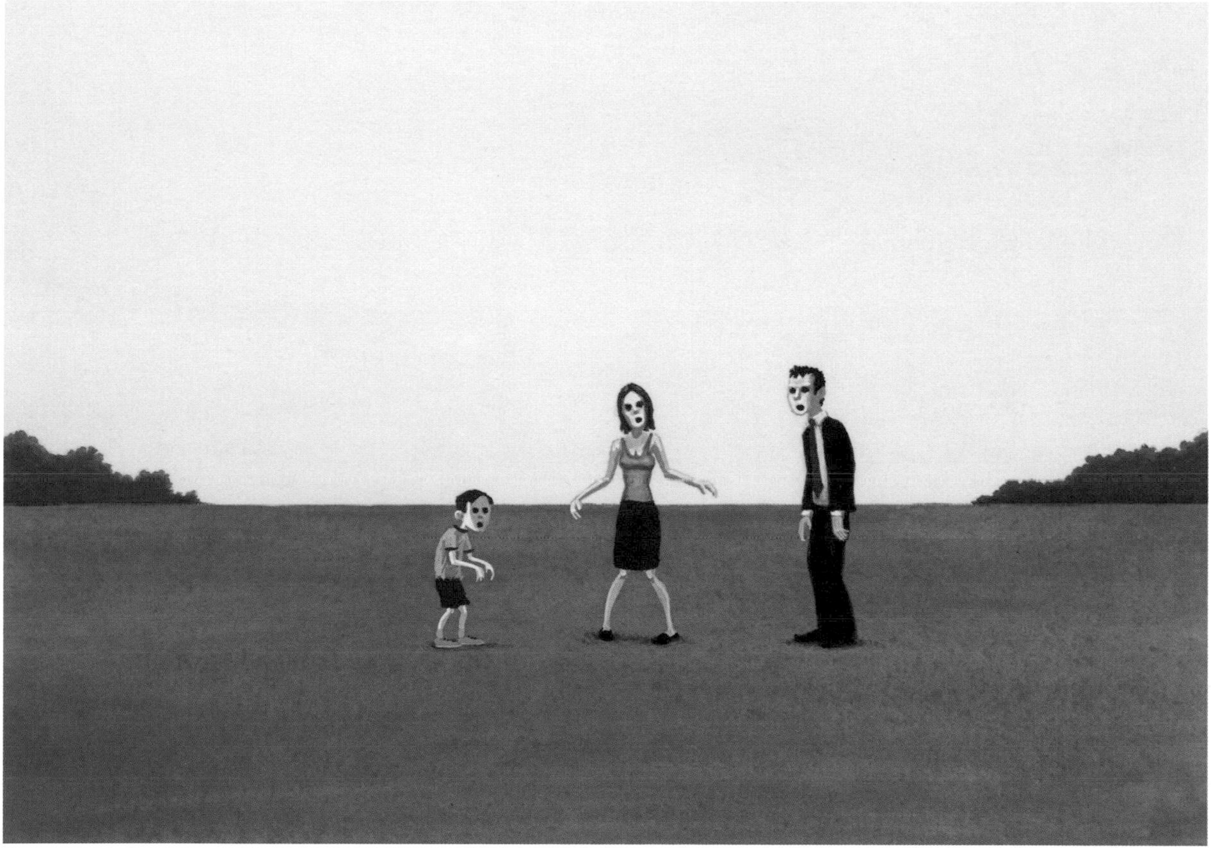

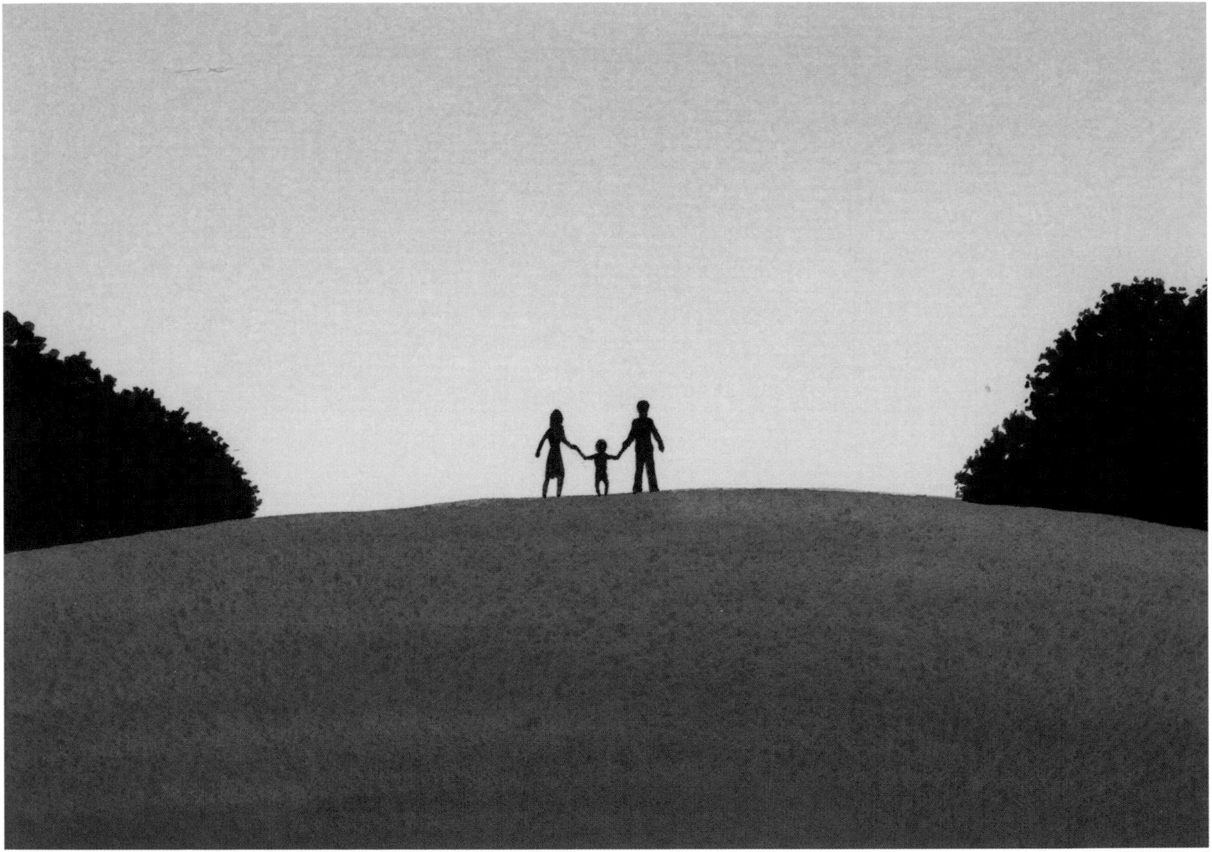